Everything Is Going To Be OK (Until It's Not)

Everything Is Going To Be OK (Until It's Not)

Georgia Garvey

Creators Publishing
Hermosa Beach

EVERYTHING IS GOING TO BE OK (UNTIL IT'S NOT)
Copyright © 2023 CREATORS PUBLISHING

All rights reserved. No part of this book may be reproduced or transmitted in any form or by any means, electronic or mechanical, including photocopying, recording or by any information storage and retrieval system, without permission in writing from the author.

Cover art by Little Shiva

CREATORS PUBLISHING
737 3rd St
Hermosa Beach, CA 90254
310-337-7003

Although the author and publisher have made every effort to ensure that the information in this book was correct at press time, the author and publisher do not assume and hereby disclaim any liability to any party for any loss, damage or disruption caused by errors or omissions, whether such errors or omissions result from negligence, accident or any other cause.

ISBN (Amazon): 9798859403530

First Edition
Printed in the United States of America
1 3 5 7 9 10 8 6 4 2

For Katerina

Contents

Introduction   1

A Little Light Reading   5

   A Birthday Gift, From My Grandmother, to the Boy She'll Never Meet   7

   The Black Hole of Death Threatens Us All. But Maybe What Comes Next Is Important, Too   11

   It's a Difficult Time for Those Seeking Easy Solutions.   14

   I'm Glad 'Maus' Was Banned   17

   Love Your Bumps Because They're What Others Love About You   20

   Living in My Fantasy, Old and Sick and Full of Life   23

   Flowers Are Blooming, and Maybe We Can, Too   26

   One Day, I'll Surrender to the Gray   29

   Middle Age, Spare Tires and Clean Plates: Something's Gotta Give   32

   What if One Picture Changed Your Life?   35

   Meeting at the Crossroads   38

   Don't Listen to Your Inner Hater: It's Not About You Anyway   41

   Endless Fertility Is Not in the Cards for Everyone   44

'Never Forget' Means First Learning What To Remember	47
I'm Off the Train to Cool Town, and I Love It	51
Forgive Others — And Yourself — For the Small Mistakes With Big Consequences	54
'The Now': All We'll Ever Have, and All We Can Ever Enjoy	57

Greek to Me — 59

Misery Can Make Magic, at Least Where Summers Are Concerned	61
The Greek 'No,' and the Long Tendrils of Old Evils	64
The Oily Reason I'm Worried About Flying	67
Banish the Chaos — At Least for a Little While	70
For the Perfect Summer Vacation, Just Add Time	73
Treasure Hunting on Vacation	76
The Ancient Greek Argument Against the Death Penalty	79
Oxi Day Reminds Us of the Value of a 'No'	81
What's Greek Easter When You Have the Other Kind?	84
Remembrance of Childhood Illnesses Past	87
Tales of the Summer Camp From Hell	90
What Have We Lost in the Exchange for Our Children's Safety?	93
Superstitions May Be Silly, but That Doesn't Mean They're Bad	96

Pandemania — 101

Daily Work Log for Garvey, Inc., Quarantine Edition	103
Why Are We in Quarantine? We're Saving the Lives of People We Will Never Meet	106
How Am I? Let's Start With the Ghost Faucet and Go From There	110

When It Comes to Vaccines, It's a Matter of Trust	113
It's the Season of Giving — Isn't It?	116
'Socialized Medicine' Can't Be Any Worse Than This	119
A Simple Proposal From a Resident of London in 1941: Let's Give Up On World War II	122
Ending Vaccine and Mask Mandates Should Be Done Slowly — and With Empathy	125
Easy Answers Elude Us as Mask and Vaccine Mandates Fall	128
During COVID-19, Parents Have Been Hung Out To Dry	131
The Pandemic Is Over but the Sickness Has Just Begun	134
No One Is Owed an Apology for Mask Mandates	137

Seasons' Greetings — 141

2020 Has Been a Tough Year. If It Makes You Feel Better, It Could Be, and Has Been, Worse	143
Hope Can Be a Powerful Thing. Let's Gift Ourselves a Bit of It This Holiday Season	146
Halloween Ghouls Have Nothing On Potty Training	150
A Gift Worth Giving Thanks For	153
The Joy of Christmas, Surpassed Only by the Joy of Christmas Past	156
The Christmas Truce of 1914 Remains a Miracle and an Inspiration	159
Springtime Brings a Blooming Bouquet — of Illness	162
Summer's Table Holds Delights Too Many To Count	165
What Am I Thankful For? Don't Make Me Say It	168
Christmas: The Season of Lying	171
The First, and Only, Honest Christmas Cookie Recipe	174
Midwestern Weather: The Worst, Other Than Everywhere Else	177

The Days Go Slowly — **181**

- Camping Is Not for Me: A Diatribe — 183
- Sometimes You Need a Dead Squirrel Disposal Service, and That's OK — 186
- In Sickness and in Health, but in 2021, Sickness Won — 189
- There Are No Monsters Here, Only Those Who Live in Darkness — 192
- Forget Writer's Block; Writer's Remorse Is the Real Pain — 195
- A Parent's Least-Favorite Sci-Fi Movie: 'Invasion of the Bed-Snatchers' — 198
- A Colonoscopy To Remember, and a Prep To Forget — 021
- When There's Nothing You Can Do, Build a Fire — 204
- Childhood Performance More of a Focus Than Ever Before — 207
- Back to School, Back to the Everyday Miseries of Childhood — 210
- Fake Eyelashes, First-Grade Math and Other Problems — 213
- Is 'M3GAN' Babysitter-Worthy? — 216
- Child-Free Adults Aren't Lazy — Parenting Has Gotten Harder — 219
- Moms, Don't Get Stuck in the Gratitude Trap — 222
- Mediocre People Need Influencers, Too — 225
- A Trip to the Aquarium — Borderline Educational, Seriously Expensive. — 228
- Crying Babies Stink, but So Do Adults Who Freak Out About Them — 231
- Technology Tricks Us, but We Are Our Own Best Gadgets — 234
- Smoking's Long, Slow Slide Into Oblivion — 237
- I've Exited Lactation Station. Now Please Tell My Doctors — 240
- The Wild, Weird History of Pets in My House — 243

Samsara and the Fine Art of Not Caring About Dirty Laundry — 246

The Firing Squad — 249

It's the Debate Over CRT That Divides Us, Not the Issue of Racism Itself — 251

Conservatives Can't Help Capitalizing On Gun Tragedies — 254

Meet the GOP of 2022: Snowflakes and Safe Spaces — 257

Leprechauns? Fine. Two Dads? Too Far — 260

For Parents, Baby Formula Is More Than Food. It's a Lifeline — 263

Student Loan Forgiveness Is Deranging Republican Politicians — 266

Who's the Queen? (And Other Fake Questions That Were Never Asked) — 269

The New Beatitudes — 272

Can Anything Stop the Wave of Conservative Fury? — 275

A New Expert Is Born Every Second — 278

High Egg Prices Really Are Just Chicken Scratch — 281

Don Lemon Was Right; Nikki Haley Is Past Her Prime — 284

If You're Giving Away Bailouts, I'll Take One, Please — 287

If My Kids Ask About Trump, Here's What I'll Say — 290

The Bizarre Failure of Conservatives To Quit When They're Ahead — 293

No Real Point to Arguing About 'Try That In A Small Town' — 296

Acknowledgments — 301
About the Author — 302

Introduction

When someone finds out I write a weekly column, they all ask the same thing:

"What's it about?"

No matter how many times I hear that question, though, it always stumps me.

Yeah, I think to myself for the hundredth time, what is it about?

I don't really have a good answer.

I suppose it's sort of about being a woman, a mother and a wife, with the multitude of frustrations, humiliations and ecstasies incumbent on those roles. It's about being overextended and underappreciated at times, but also overjoyed at and aware of the gifts that present themselves.

The column is also about life, at least life in the time and place where I live it - full of the general weirdness of being alive in the United States in 2023, in the wake of a global pandemic, with our memories of those bizarre experiences both fading and warping, the way memories will do. It's about the way people seem crueler, further away from each other, even though that's only an illusion. We're still as close as we want to be, if only we'd open our eyes to see it.

Occasionally, in my writing, there's an ill-advised foray into politics or current events, when I can't stop myself from finger-wagging. When I can, I remember that the world will be just fine if I keep my mouth shut about oh, let's say, the M&M spokescandies' high heels. The world is lousy with opinions, after all, and usually they're not worth the paper a Trump NFT is printed on. As Robert Duvall's character Bernie says in the movie The Paper, "We reek of opinions."

Now that I think about it, I guess, I'm mostly writing an advice column - only the advice travels in a circle, from me back to me.

My writings are a conversation with myself, and often they're a journal of my never-ending battle - one fought by the week, by the day, sometimes by the minute - to avoid living either in the future (with worry) or in the past (with guilt).

We all have a "thing," a lifelong struggle, and that's mine.

I write as a kind of therapy on that front. It's a teasing out of my insecurities and my fears.

Should I keep dyeing my gray hair, long past the point at which it's aesthetically or financially prudent just because stopping informs the world that I am no longer 23 years old?

Should I feel decrepit for thinking that the Lollapalooza band lineup looks like a bowlful of random nouns puked up by an AI chatbot?

Should I live in fear that one day, someone I love will die?

When I write those questions out, maybe other people feel the same way. Maybe they enjoy reading my musings, the topics I pull each week from my giant mental hat. But usually, I'm working something out for myself.

And as I'm chewing over these matters - big and small - I often wind up advising myself.

One day, for example, I was talking to my therapist about my grinding dread that some horrible fate will befall my kids or my husband or me or any number of other friends and family members.

I don't remember his exact words, which is odd considering how the sentiment stuck in my brain like a burr on fur, but I remember him saying something a lot like this:

"Everything's going to be OK, until it isn't."

It was morbidly frank but also profoundly reassuring.

Because, my friends, the meteor is coming for us all, whether we like it or not. We cannot delay or predict the time of its arrival. The only choice we get is how to spend the time we have before it hits.

I do think about death a lot. But, strangely, writing and talking about it reduces the fear, like opening a valve on a pressurized container.

That trait is one my son and I share, and there have been times when he was feeling particularly concerned about death, and we talked about it. We talked about how cool it would be if, in one of the infinite solar systems in the infinitely massive universe, there were a planet just like Earth, with a boy on it just like him and a mom on it just like me, except on that planet, no one died.

Maybe we'll go there one day, I said. Or maybe we're living there already, and we just don't know it. Maybe we're all living the continuations of other lives. There are so many possibilities.

Death, like life, is a mystery that never gets solved.

If we're lucky, we get some time, though, to try to unravel it, and I'm determined to spend mine thinking, and writing, and sharing those thoughts and words with anyone who wants to read them. Maybe that's what this column is.

Because one day, the meteor will come for me, too.

But until then, everything's going to be OK.

A Little Light Reading

A Birthday Gift, From My Grandmother, to the Boy She'll Never Meet

March 25, 2017

Later this month, my son will turn a year old.

We'll throw a party — grander than some but probably more laid-back than most - eat gyros and cupcakes, talk about how squirmy he is, how cute his four teeth are. It promises to be thoroughly normal. His start in life, though, was another matter.

Seven years ago, my husband and I started trying to have a baby.

There were endocrinologists, needles, hormones, plane flights and procedures. It all finally, strangely, worked, and I wound up pregnant, only to be greeted at 5 weeks with a kind of bleeding that doesn't seem compatible with life.

Somehow, though, that scrap of cells persisted, hanging on despite continued growth scans that showed he wasn't getting as big, as quickly, as the doctors expected.

Early on my husband bought a fetal monitor, the kind doctors tell you not to get because it'll drive you crazy. We listened to it as often as we could justify, usually once a day, to hold back our fears between appointments.

Like clockwork, I'd go to doctor visits and lie down on the paper cover, only exhaling at the tiniest of victories.

Heartbeat, breath. Amniotic fluid, breath. Spinal column,

breath.

Eventually, the baby was diagnosed with intrauterine growth restriction, a phrase that conjured up images of my son trapped inside me in fetal solitary confinement. The high-risk obstetricians, coldly precise geniuses, were kind but mostly unrelenting in their pessimism, or neutralism at the very most. They occasionally used words like "fetal demise" and "stillbirth."

At one point, after my husband had asked with desperation if there was anything we could do, one specialist suggested we go home and pray, if we were "the praying types."

I thought about my older brother, who had died seven hours after he was born with the umbilical cord wrapped around his neck. I knew there was a cosmic dice game afoot, one I couldn't anticipate, let alone control.

So, I talked to my grandmother, a fierce Greek peasant whose bones are interred in a family crypt at the top of a mountain.

I could not imagine a more dreadful champion than Yia-Yia, black scarf tied around her head and fingers twisted from working in the fields.

She loved me terribly, once lopping the head off a rooster after it pecked me too many times. But she also yelled at me when I slipped on the rocks in the village in my pink patent-leather sandals, shaking my shoulder to tell me that those pretty shoes were dangerously stupid.

I decided it was her I wanted wherever my son's fate was being decided. I knew she wouldn't be above cheating, lying, stealing. She would know that anything that could be done should, but that one must have common sense, must accept any consequence, fair or foul.

At 22 weeks, the doctors told us to prepare for a delivery at any point.

Each day, which I began and ended with a quick chat with Yia-Yia, was a chip away at the time we were told to expect in the neonatal intensive care unit. When I felt him kick, a short stab of joy would lift my heart. He was still alive, still moving.

Finally, at 30 weeks, the doctor said no more work, even from home. I was allowed a couple of hours sitting down for my baby shower that Sunday. For some reason, I wore black.

In the 33rd week, there was a drop in his heartbeat, and I was admitted to Evanston Hospital. I would have a C-section, because he was breech but also due to his size.

"How small will he be?" my husband asked the neonatologist. She motioned with her hands, creating a dainty cup.

"So, about the size of a squirrel," he said. "Without the tail."

The contractions began shortly thereafter, slight at first but building. Later that night, after a giant squeeze, I heard a pop and felt a gush of fluid. I felt him moving inside me, and it seemed wrong, as if he were inside a plastic bag, suffocating.

The contractions turned wrenching. The painkillers came, and for about 15 minutes, I felt a blissful loosening of the screws in my brain that had been overtightened for so long.

Too soon, the medication wore off.

"I just want them to take him out," I said to my husband.

Finally, the obstetrician from my home practice walked into the room. She looked cheerful and confident. I held on to that, and to the knowledge that Yia-Yia was breaking kneecaps for me in heaven. I asked her for the strength to deal with whatever would come.

In the operating room, I was laid on the table and strapped down. I felt the doctors rummage around in my abdomen.

I was virtually swimming in a pool of fear.

Then, they pulled something out and I craned my neck to see a bawling red mass under a heating lamp. People were crowded around it, and I saw a stray foot, a tiny hand, through their busy limbs.

"He's fine," someone said.

They walked him over and held him out to me. His eyes were huge, swollen and red-rimmed, as if he'd been awoken too early. The doctor said he was 3 pounds, 4 ounces - 15 ounces more than expected.

I didn't cry. I didn't feel happiness or frustration or relief or sadness. I just wanted them to take him to the NICU, to check him, to do whatever he needed.

I touched the baby fleetingly, silently promising that I'd do better the next time I saw him.

There would be no pictures of grinning parents, no sublime breast-feeding moment, no cuddling him close.

But Yia-Yia's voice sounded in my head, telling me not to feel sorry for myself. She gave birth to my father, after all, on a straw floor in a one-room hovel. I had a son, and he was alive.

It was more than you should have hoped for, Yia-Yia might have said, and far more than many get.

(c) 2023 Chicago Tribune. All rights reserved. Distributed by Tribune Content Agency, LLC

The Black Hole of Death Threatens Us All. But Maybe What Comes Next Is Important, Too

September 20, 2020

    I was making dinner when I heard the scream, a wail from the living room, where my two sons were watching TV while I cooked.

    I ran in, saw our 4-year-old, tears collecting in his eyes.

    "What's wrong?" I asked, looking around, thinking I'd find a bruised shin, a spider, something scary. On the television was a children's science video explaining how black holes are made.

    "Does it hurt the star?" my son asked, a pleading tone to his voice.

    "Hurt the star?" I stammered, glancing back at the screen.

    "Does it hurt when it dies?" he asked. I remembered, then, some of my high school science about the formation of a black hole, how it's created after the death of a massive star. The video was smack in the middle of describing the bright supernova created after the star's collapse.

    At moments like these, I'm limited as a parent - not just by my ignorance of stellar life cycles but also by my desire not to have him sympathize too deeply with everything from stars in the far reaches of space to the broccoli on his plate. I don't want him to be paralyzed by empathy, become unable to let negative energy exist without absorbing it. I try to find shortcuts out of unwinnable conversations, ways not to have to admit that existence is fleeting and that, yes, honey, death does, indeed, come for us all.

    So I tried to explain that stars don't have feelings like people or animals do, mumbled something about stars being just balls of gas and rock.

"They don't have souls or hearts or brains," I said, though he remained unconvinced. In his mind, the star had been a thing, a complex and beautiful thing, and now it was no more. It had died, and by all rights, he seemed to be saying, we should be sad.

I tried, instead, to focus on the black hole, the remnant of the dead star, the powerful and shocking aftermath of its demise. That seemed to help, and strangely, it also reminded me of COVID-19, Ruth Bader Ginsburg and the koliva I'm making.

Koliva, for the uninitiated, is a funeral dish often made by Greek Orthodox Christians. The ingredients vary, but it starts with wheat berries, sugar, parsley and often includes almonds, pomegranate seeds or raisins. The inspiration for the dish, according to Fr. Chrysanthos Kerkeres of St. George Greek Orthodox Church in Chicago, is the resurrection of Jesus and the Bible verse of John 12:24.

"Truly, truly, I say to you," it reads, "unless a grain of wheat falls into the earth and dies, it remains alone; but if it dies, it bears much fruit."

It's a way of saying that though death is always tragic, there is unquestionably, without doubt, more afterward, whether you believe in God or stupendously large black holes or nothing at all.

Koliva, the resurrection of Jesus, supernovas, black holes - they all can contribute to fulfilling our yearning to make sense out of death, to give meaning to tragedy.

Think about the death of a star: When a red supergiant has used up the last of its fuel, when it collapses under the weight of its own gravity, a brilliant flash of light - a supernova - explodes, blasting fragments of the star out into the universe. What's left is a magnificent black hole, a body with gravitational pull so strong it can pull in everything around it, including light.

It comforts me to know that when a star dies, it sends pieces of itself out into the universe, changing its surroundings and contributing to the birth of other planets and stars. And after the transformation of death happens, what's left behind can sometimes be even more powerful.

Scientists believe that a supermassive black hole might live at the middle of every galaxy. Our own Milky Way is home to Sagittarius

A*. Some scientists, including Professor James Unwin at the University of Illinois at Chicago, recently suggested it's even possible there could be a black hole at the far reaches of our solar system, one created during the Big Bang, at the start of all time and space.

Maybe a black hole - a death, in other words - lies at the center, the start of all things. Maybe death is at the nexus of everything that matters.

Now, back to the koliva: I decided to make the dish for after the death of my grandmother, who though not an Orthodox Christian was a person of faith. But I'm not just making it for her.

I'm also making it for the more than 200,000 people who have died in the U.S. from coronavirus. I'm making it for DaJore Wilson. I'm making it for George Floyd. Perhaps that sounds cloying, patronizing, melodramatic, and maybe it is all of those things. But it helps me to think that their deaths will not be in vain, that their passings will, in the parlance of the Bible, bear fruit.

I don't know whether Ginsburg, who was Jewish, would mind being included. Somehow I doubt it.

Either way, when I take a bite of the koliva, and remember all those who've lost their lives this year, I will think of them as one of those grains of wheat. Though they've fallen, I hope, they might still have more to contribute. Maybe they'll be like a dying star.

Perhaps their most powerful contributions, in fact, are yet to come.

Thank you to Professor James Unwin for providing invaluable information about black holes.

(c) 2023 Pioneer Press. All rights reserved. Distributed by Tribune Content Agency, LLC

It's a Difficult Time for Those Seeking Easy Solutions

September 26, 2022

"What's the topic this week?" my husband asked as I settled down to write my column today. "Kiev?"

I groaned.

"Ugh, no. I'm no expert on Ukraine."

I'm not a diplomat or a foreign policy whiz, and my performance on a Wordle-ish geography game I've been playing has so far been unimpressive.

My sight recognition of countries like Suriname and Micronesia, while probably better than average, embarrasses me so much I usually cheat and Google.

I mean, what do I know about Ukraine?

I can't even understand what this is about — why Russian dictator Vladimir Putin referenced decades-old squabbles in his speech announcing the deployment of a "peacekeeping" force to the region.

"What nonsense is this?" I thought, listening to him complain about Vladimir Lenin not getting enough credit for creating Ukraine. He sounded like an old man, full of bile and enamored with the sound of his grievances. I wandered away from the TV the same way I'd wander away from someone complaining about how kids don't get hit enough these days.

Putin's putting the band back together, only the band in this case is the Soviet Union and he's occupying sovereign countries and killing people to do it.

But what we should do about it — there I'm out of my depth.

I'm still trying to figure out whether to let our son go to school maskless, debating endlessly with myself about whether it's worth the risk to him and others.

Our school district held a meeting recently to vote on the topic, and my son came home that day chanting, "mask optional, mask optional, mask optional" like a tiny bureaucratic automaton. The teachers had talked to them about what it might be like to see some of your friends wearing masks and others not.

They did a skillful job of impressing upon the kids that the right decision for them might not be the right decision for another person.

"We shouldn't tell our friends they're bad for wearing a mask or not wearing one, honey," I said, worried my little test proctor of a child would feel it incumbent upon him to correct his kindergarten classmates.

"Geez, I know that, Mom," he said, sighing, already sick of the subject.

I didn't have any good answers, feeling torn between what's admittedly a minor risk of illness and death for our son and the possibility of extending the lifespan of a disease we already have borne too long.

What should we do?

I don't know. I couldn't even figure out what to do the other day watching a nanny put a small child in an extended time out, more than an hour long at least, as he was forced to watch the other kids play and gambol around him.

It's not my place, I kept telling myself, sick at the look of shame on his face. *What, even, would I do?*

A couple of times, I murmured a mild comment about the length of the punishment but couldn't bring myself to interfere more.

I don't know the back story, I thought. *I don't know that kid or his parents or his nanny.*

"Children are in a war zone right now," my husband reminded me when I told him how I couldn't stop thinking about the boy. "There are worse things than an hourlong time out."

Later in bed, though, I cried. Not for the child — who didn't seem injured or hungry or sick — but out of helplessness. Ukraine, COVID, even a boy sitting across the room from me — I'm not certain of anything other than the wrongness I feel.

But what to do? I asked, getting no answer.

What to do, what to do, what to do?

I'm Glad 'Maus' Was Banned

March 12, 2022

I owe a thank you to the Tennessee school board that banned "Maus."

After the McMinn County School Board voted to remove the graphic novel, the first of its kind to win the Pulitzer Prize, from its eighth-grade curriculum, I finally got around to reading the book, which had been on my list for years.

I'd never before been in the mood for a Holocaust-themed comic book, but after it made national news, I figured I'd see what all the fuss was about.

And was "Maus" good? Oh, *yes*.

Once I started reading it, I couldn't stop. I found myself propping the book open while I cooked dinner, refusing to put it down at night when my eyes drooped, wanting to get in a few more pages.

The author, Art Spiegelman, found a way to impart both the scale and the immediacy of the Holocaust. Inside the book, I discovered meditations on art, trauma and life. I thought about what it means to be a writer, what it means to be a child and a parent, what it means to be a human.

I also found some strange parallels to my own story.

When I read about the death of Spiegelman's older brother, I thought of my own brother, who died shortly after birth, and the way a child's death reshapes a parent.

And Spiegelman's father, a survivor of Auschwitz, reminded me in small ways of my own dad, who escaped crushing poverty in Greece before immigrating to the United States.

I asked myself whether the traits both men seemed to share — a powerful value of blood ties and a thrift in all things, even emotion — were created by their circumstances or were inborn traits that helped them survive.

I asked myself whether the book's dehumanization of its characters — depicting Jewish people as mice, Germans as cats, Americans as dogs, Poles as pigs — made it easier or harder to understand how Nazis could perpetrate such horrors.

How can I persuade the uninitiated to read it other than to say, "Don't you want to know what all the fuss is about, too?"

Clearly, plenty do.

The book rocketed to the top of bestseller lists, and The New York Times reported on high schoolers passing copies of "Maus" to each other.

Turns out, dropping the book from the curriculum made "Maus" cooler than any forced reading ever could.

I do wonder, though, if "Maus" is wasted on the young.

I find myself remembering how my first reading of "A Tale of Two Cities" failed to impress. My only memory of it in ninth grade is getting a test question wrong on the significance of Madame Defarge's knitting.

Later, as an adult, I idly picked up a copy of "A Tale of Two Cities" and read the first few lines.

"It was the best of times, it was the worst of times ..."

All the most important stages in our lives are, I thought.

Then, I kept reading, barreling through the book in a few days. I couldn't stop.

It's since become one of my favorites, and I've reread it multiple times. The novel's plotting, characters and themes shock me anew each time.

Could I have understood that as a child? Could I have appreciated it? I don't think so.

Maybe it's the same with "Maus." Maybe, by making a stink over the book, the school board gave more people a reason to find it and to love it, as I did. Maybe kids won't read "Maus" when they're too young to fully appreciate it but will return, years later, to find the treasures within.

I hope so.

I do know, though, that's what happened to me, and for that, I owe that Tennessee school board a debt of gratitude.

Thank you for closing your minds, so that I might open mine.

The book wasn't written for you anyway.

Love Your Bumps Because They're What Others Love About You

April 2, 2022

On my right hand, between the first and second knuckles, tucked away inside my fingers, sits a tiny bump.

For the first four decades of my life, I had no idea it existed.

Even now, I don't know what it is: beauty mark, mole or some other kind of miniature flaw. It doesn't much matter anyway, as small and insignificant as it is.

But in the last three years, since the birth of our youngest son, the bump has become not just visible but important.

"Can I touch the bump?" he asked, at first, though now I put my hand in his at nighttime without him asking. He pets my hand, lightly, almost meditatively, as he drinks his milk or when he wakes up from a nightmare and needs comforting.

When we hold hands crossing the street, he quickly grabs my right hand before our other son can get there.

"It's my favorite hand," he says, "because of the bump."

I've often marveled how that tiny imperfection is his favorite part of me.

Many times, I've looked at that bump and thought of how, when I was a child, I disliked my name.

My first name, Georgia, was odd, in the worst way.

The world around me was full of Heathers and Jennifers

and Melissas, and whenever I met someone, they'd make the same lame joke about my siblings being named "North Dakota" or "Wyoming." "Georgia" also means "farmer," and I could think of nothing less glamorous than working in dirt.

My last name was Evdoxiadis, a tongue-twister of uncertain but profound ethnicity to anyone who wasn't, themselves, Greek.

As far as pronunciation went, forget it.

Reading my name on the class list, a teacher's eyes would widen. They'd sometimes stammer out an attempt.

"Ev — ox — ee — aye — dis," was a common mangling.

Of course, there also were jokes about my name sounding like diseases and how I learned to spell it in kindergarten, unfunny jokes too numerous to recount here.

I've had more than one person simply refuse to try, which, in some ways, was a bit of a relief.

My name, first and last, branded me as a foreigner, an outsider, someone who'd never be the blond cheerleader, the '80s movie love interest. Instead, I was a greasy Greek who ate weird food and had an even weirder name.

I tried to erase that weirdness in my fantasies, created a world where I corrected that flaw of a name.

In junior high, I wrote what would now be considered fanfic about working as a Rolling Stone reporter. In it, my first name was glamorous and strong, like Veronica or Vivian, my last name bland and white, like Clark.

When I married, though, I changed my name and my feelings started to shift.

I often missed my Greek last name, the sticker that advertised me as a stranger, an outsider and an immigrant.

I'd long grown to love my first name. It's uncommon, and I now value that. It's also a name that I share, in a masculine form, with my great-grandfather, my father and now my youngest son. It's a bond to my history, and to my future.

I didn't see it at the time, but my name was always interesting, weird and a little cool.

And, like the bump on my hand, whether I liked it or not, it was part of me.

I wish I'd known back then that my flaws, the places where I fell short, would be, as I aged, what I and others would most love about me.

Because our most interesting features are always the bumps. They're the places, not where we're the same, but where we diverge. And in the end, they're the only parts that matter.

They're memorable. They're worthy of pride.

Our differences are not just beautiful. They're something even more important: They're us.

Living in My Fantasy, Old and Sick and Full of Life

April 30, 2022

In one of my favorite fantasies, I'm old.

I'm sitting at my kitchen table, wrapped in a well-loved but somewhat ratty bathrobe, leisurely sipping coffee and taking bites of buttered toast slathered in cherry jam. Outside, the sun shines and birds chirp.

I flip through a fat newspaper, passing up all the stories that look too depressing or too long. I linger on book and movie reviews, then do the crossword puzzle in pen.

At no point in this reverie does anything remarkable happen.

What makes this mundane dream so relaxing, so marvelous, is what's *not* there.

There are no thoughts of work, children or home; my most important successes and biggest mistakes in those regards have concluded. I'm not worried about gaining weight or going gray because, on both fronts, the fight is over. I look like what I look like, and my accomplishments, or lack thereof, are what they are.

What a relief.

Now, before you start, I know aging isn't all coffee and crossword puzzles, and the elderly have plenty of troubles, but still, it won't be all bad, will it?

Catching COVID wasn't all bad, either.

After two years of successfully eluding it, the coronavirus finally, recently, caught me.

Or, more accurately, I caught it.

I'm vaccinated and boosted, and I was never in the highest-risk categories, so I wasn't terrified. And though it made me nervous, in some strange way, I was relieved.

The coughing, fever, body aches and chills were all profoundly unpleasant, and I'm sure my husband didn't feel much pleasure as he did all the cooking, cleaning and child care.

But as I lay in bed, I thought to myself how at least the days of feeling hunted, like a leopard trying to avoid the working end of Trump Jr.'s assault rifle, were over. There was no point in worrying about catching COVID anymore.

What would be, would be.

In the insistency of illness, I couldn't think about much more than how my body felt. I was tired but couldn't sleep, so I turned on TV shows that didn't demand much. I dozed to mysteries and reality shows. I drank and ate what I liked, which wasn't usually much, but there was no guilt in any of it.

It reminded me of being in the hospital, newly postpartum, when the hard work of pregnancy had concluded and the harder work of parenthood hadn't fully begun.

My mental state got worse, though, once I started to recover from COVID. Because then the worries crept in, and in my weakened physical state, it was harder to fight them.

What about the kids and school?
Will my husband catch it from me?
What to do about all that laundry?

But eventually I realized that I could still, in some ways, live in that place, that imaginary place where I was sick, or old, or recovering from childbirth.

I could live in the place where I didn't worry about when the sheets had last been changed. I could cut myself a break on how much TV the kids watched. I could lose weight another day.

It didn't have to be today. And, if I'm honest, with most of my fears and worries, it didn't have to be ever.

Because when the day comes that I'm actually old, actually sitting with my coffee, actually wearing that ratty bathrobe and actually looking at that sunshine, I don't anticipate regretting the early release of any fears.

What has been, has been. What will be, will be.

I imagine that I'll then think, only, about the marvelous and mundane right now.

And what a relief that will be.

Flowers Are Blooming, and Maybe We Can, Too

May 14, 2022

Everywhere I go, I see tulips.

In the Midwest, we had a godawful April.

The umbrellas barely had a chance to dry from one rainstorm before the next downpour started. Day after day: wet, cold, miserable.

Half of the people I know (including half of the people in my house) got COVID last month. The few who didn't succumb caught a weekslong upper respiratory infection that dragged on like an Allman Brothers song.

The Easter candy in the house seemed to be multiplying, so I decided to help the kids "finish it off." In unrelated news, I gained 5 pounds.

I also finalized their plans for summer vacation, which, somehow, only managed to make it feel even further off.

"It'll never be warm enough to swim in the pool," I thought, miserably, as I paid for the summer park district passes.

Trips to the gas station started costing $50, and we began regularly dropping $200 at the grocery store.

I used to hate hearing the word "COVID." Now it's "inflation."

Now, I'm not pretending to be some yokel who doesn't understand price increases. I get why things cost more. It makes sense.

After all, everyone quit or lost their job during the pandemic. Everyone who could moved. Everyone who could started working from home. We contracted, willfully, withdrew into ourselves and our homes and our families, and that's all very natural during a time when millions of people are dying.

And with fewer of us going around, going out, extending ourselves outward, companies have had to pay more. Hence, we have to pay more — dramatically more.

Still, though, it doesn't feel like our politicians responded in an equally dramatic fashion.

There was no dramatic increase in the minimum wage. There have been no dramatic efforts to improve health care coverage or increase the availability of child care.

There have been no job training programs, no help for those who want to start small businesses.

It's as if, one day, everyone in Washington decided that it was time for people to get back to normal.

"OK, leave your house," they seemed to say. "Buy things, go to work, take your kids to day care, the same as before."

The only problem was, nothing was the same as before.

I'm still waiting for people to stop arguing about critical race theory and gender theory and notice the only real issue: Neither Democratic nor Republican politicians will take any action to help anyone unless they are forced to do it.

They will not reform the corrupt campaign finance system in this country.

They will not increase wages, improve health care, subsidize child care or find ways to strengthen the job prospects of Americans.

They won't because they don't have to.

They need only make the appropriate noises about banned books and abortion and transgender issues, the noises those on their side want them to make, and everyone's placated for another news cycle.

They don't actually have to do anything.

In April, this seemed horribly predestined. As I slogged through the mud to drag my two shivering children to school, there was nothing I could do, nothing any of us could do, about the chill, about the rain.

But in May, everywhere I go, I see tulips.

They've been hiding all winter, deep underground. As the sun has emerged, chasing away the cold and snow, the flowers can bloom.

They can wake up, see the world for what it is, what it has always been.

But, somehow, though my world hasn't changed, the tulips have made it better.

It's their time, now, and maybe one day soon, it will be our time, as well.

Maybe one day, it will be May in America.

One Day, I'll Surrender to the Gray

June 18, 2022

I got my first gray hair at 16.

It wasn't entirely unexpected. My dad — who also went prematurely gray — had dyed his hair since I was a child.

Even so, it made me nervous to find that silvery strand, seeing decades' worth of hair dye in my future, stretching out in expensive hair salon appointments as far as the eye could see.

I decided, at first, to treat it as fun. I dyed my hair shades of red, brown, black and blond. Sometimes I'd have highlights, other times none. The experimentation was a game, and for most of my teens and 20s, I enjoyed it.

I never minded if someone found out I had gray hairs because I knew, and I knew they knew, too, that no matter how many gray hairs I had, I was young. Plus, I was dying my hair, so no one knew unless I told them.

"Why don't you let it grow out?" my husband asked when we first started dating. "It might look cool."

I laughed, certain that he didn't want to date a woman who looked 20 years older than she was any more than I wanted to be one.

As I got older, though, things changed.

It wasn't quite so funny to know that, left unmolested, my hair would make me look older than I was. Eventually, I hit the age where my contemporaries started going gray, too, and the advanced stage of my gray hair made me feel less unique and more frumpy.

Dying my hair became more of a chore, too.

Even a couple of weeks after an appointment at a hair salon, I can see grays peeking through at the hairline. Within a month or two, the full state of things is clear.

I've started thinking more about my dad, who at 70 years old still dyes his hair jet-black, covering his white moustache hairs as well. He used to dye the hair on his arms and chest, even, and I remember him sitting in the dye, waiting for it to set, and wondering why he bothered.

"Don't you'd think you look better with gray hair?" I asked him once.

"No," he said. "I think I'd look old."

Now that I'm firmly in middle age, I understand the fear, the worry that keeps you trying to stop youth's retreat.

It's not that you won't look beautiful. It's that you won't look beautiful in the same way. And the way you used to look beautiful — the unlined, un-old, un-gray way — is the way that's desirable, that's sexy.

With advancing age comes a degree of invisibility, and for those who have spent so many years being seen, it can be like a drug. It can be tough to kick.

I was never a model, never the most stunning woman in the room, but when you're young, you're beautiful, whether you know it or not. Sometimes you find the beauty in a way that others recognize, wearing the "right" clothes and makeup, doing your hair the "right" way. Especially for women, it can require an extraordinary amount of effort.

At some point, though, everyone must decide whether to keep up the fight. How long and how hard do we want to struggle against the invincible foe?

I've been looking at my hair recently and considering surrender.

Would it be so horrible to look old? Would it be OK — maybe even good — to see if there's beauty to be found over the hill?

I have an appointment with my hair stylist coming up, and I'm planning what to say.

In the past, it's been all about hiding. Covering up.

This time, I'd like to figure out a way to be beautiful, only *with* the gray hair.

Middle Age, Spare Tires and Clean Plates: Something's Gotta Give

July 2, 2022

I'm too young to have an arthritic hip.
That's what I tell myself while I rub prescription gel in to numb a sharp, insistent pain that is most certainly not from arthritis.

I'm too young to need reading glasses, let alone go up in magnification, I say as I shop online for 1.5 strength "cheaters."

These lidocaine patches must be for someone else, I think while the lady at the pharmacy rings them up.

"Is there nothing I can do to slow this mudslide into decrepitude?" I ask the doctor as I sit in the disposable shorts they'd given me for the hip X-ray. The shorts have an elastic waistband, balloon out wide enough that a strong upward breeze could send me into flight and feel disturbingly comfortable. I consider sneaking them home in my purse.

"You could always lose weight," the doctor answers, slowly, bracing for impact.

I'm not insulted, though I am depressed.

What's the secret? What's the pill, the exercise, the specialty diet that works where others don't?

"Count calories. When we get older, we can't eat the same way we used to."

My mind wanders back, wistfully, to high school, when I'd have an orange juice and a Nutty Buddy from the vending machine for breakfast. At least it was high in vitamin C.

Now I have to eat like a grown-up.

I've gone on a ... sorry, hold on, just having trouble getting the word out ... *diet.*

The word makes me shiver. Its very sound makes me feel older.

I've fought it long and hard, mostly because of the general unfairness of the whole thing. It just seems cruel, that my body would work against me like this.

I know evolution's to blame, that when we were cavemen and cavewomen, the tendency to store extra pounds could mean the difference between surviving the winter and becoming a dead branch on the family tree.

But it's 2022 and I live in the United States, and my body still holds on to unnecessary fat as if the ready supply of woolly mammoth meat could dry up at any minute.

There are many good reasons why I've put on weight over the years — IVF, then pregnancy, then the pandemic. Not fair, not fair, not fair.

Still, true. Railing against the unfairness hasn't dissolved a single pound.

I've been on a decadelong strike against reality, but now it's time to change. It's time to eat more vegetables and less meat, to pass up the French fries and cinnamon rolls — if not forever, at least more frequently.

The only problem is, sometimes it's tough to convince my stomach that it wouldn't just be better to eat the ice cream and die sooner. (My stomach is stupid, you see.)

It can help to look at my kids, but occasionally, that has the opposite effect. There they sit, smugly thin, refusing to eat another bite of mac and cheese.

"You can't have any candy until you finish your pizza," my husband tells them.

I made Nicoise salad the other night: seared tuna, Dijon

dressing and perfectly cooked vegetables.

It was healthy, and, therefore, I resented it.

Not because it wasn't delicious but because it wasn't what I would have chosen 25 years ago, when there was no such thing as cholesterol and my meals were limited only by my appetite.

I guess it's not the food I'm hungry for.

I wonder if the trick is to realize that those lost years can't be found in donuts. Maybe Nicoise salads *are* the fountain of youth.

At least, that is, until I look in the medicine cabinet and see those lidocaine patches.

But I shouldn't worry. After all, they're for someone else, aren't they?

What if One Picture Changed Your Life?

July 9, 2022

Let's say you've seen a picture, one that shows a curly-haired toddler, his eyes glazed with confusion as he sits on a stranger's lap.

Let's say the Highland Park police release the photo publicly, disseminating it far and wide, trying to find the boy's parents. Maybe you wonder, "What could have kept his parents from him?"

Let's say you imagine what that boy saw and heard, in the moments after the shooting started — the noises and the smells, the running and the screams. There's blood on the boy's legs, on his socks and shoes, and perhaps it occurs to you how that blood got there.

Let's say you keep thinking about that child being shielded from gunfire by his dying father. You might try not to remember but be unable to forget the words of a good Samaritan doctor who described the aftermath. Maybe you can't even type those words now, for fear they will infect another person's brain as they have infected yours.

But, if you saw that picture, those images, those thoughts might be burned into your mind and your soul — forever. Once you saw it, maybe your eyes could never be closed again.

Maybe you abhor the taking of innocent life. If, to you, the life of a child matters more than unlimited personal freedom, you might wonder, doesn't that little boy count? Don't his parents?

Maybe you believe in the Bible, the Quran or the Torah. You might ask yourself why we sacrifice human lives on the altar of guns. Aren't we commanded to put nothing before God?

Maybe you are a parent or a grandparent, a dog lover or a neighbor, an environmentalist or an activist, a firefighter or a teacher, a police officer or a friend. Maybe you have a heart: Shouldn't that photograph, the look on that boy's shell-shocked face, break it?

Or maybe you care for no one but yourself. Well, then, you — *don't you matter?*

What about your right to go to school, a movie theater, a church, a country music concert, a Fourth of July parade without being murdered?

What about you?

Do you deserve this? Do any of us? Do we deserve to live in a country where the sounds we hear on July 4 could be celebratory fireworks or the random automatic gunfire of a mass murderer?

Do we want this country to be the kind of place where we arm killers with military-grade weapons?

Do we want to watch more children become orphans, more parents bury their children, more communities mourn? Do we want to sacrifice one more precious life for the gun lobby's benefit?

It has become clear that the politicians will not decide for us.

They will not deliver what we do not order.

We have left it to them for the last 8 years, after the assault weapons ban expired on Sept. 13, 2004, and they have told us in no uncertain terms that if we do not insist, they will not act.

So, maybe, the next step might be to weigh the choices.

Maybe you ask yourself, which is more important: Our freedom to own assault weapons, or one little boy wearing bloody socks?

Or maybe the choice has already been made for you.

You've seen the picture, and it lives inside you, propels you forward.

You're fed up with thinking and praying, remembering that faith without works is dead. You don't want there to be more horror without at least trying to prevent it.

Maybe the only path is action.

Maybe the only time is now.

Maybe the only person is you.

Meeting at the Crossroads

October 1, 2022

Autumn, like all good art, is about death.

That's what I found myself thinking as I read the comments on Bone Thugs-N-Harmony's "Tha Crossroads" video on YouTube.

Bone Thugs-N-Harmony is a rap group from the 1990s, though I'm mostly familiar with their oeuvre based on what I could pick up through the walls separating my teenage room from that of my little brother. He blasted the group's "Thuggish Ruggish Bone" so loudly and so many times in a row that it seemed at the time to be punitive, or maybe an exotic torture method.

But the other day, I tripped and fell into an internet black hole and wound up watching '90s music videos for almost an hour.

In the one for "Tha Crossroads," an Angel of Death-type figure gathers up the souls of the departed, including a baby and a young man mourned by his mother. It's a sad song, depressing even, talking of meeting lost loved ones at the crossroads and at one point offering a plaintive "I don't wanna die."

It touches a nerve, and reading the comments were like peeking into the thoughts of funeral mourners. There were lamentations for beloved family members and even a post from someone dying of bone cancer.

"I will miss the loved ones I will leave behind but look forward to being reunited with the ones I have lost," he wrote.

I've been thinking a lot about death lately, as fall finds its foothold and the weather changes. For there's beauty in the season, but that beauty is rooted in endings, in the passing away of what was once sweet. There's Halloween and fallen leaves and the promise of winter's cold embrace — they remind us of one of the few experiences that all human beings will share.

Far smarter people than me have spoken far more eloquently about the links between death and fall, but what struck me was the way so many of us love the season of autumn, perhaps *because* it reminds us of dying.

For me, this fall has particular meaning as I enter the second half of my life, my autumn season. My birthday approaches and once it's here, I can no longer pretend to be in my summer prime.

My hair is graying and my neck is sagging, and if I ever forget my age, my knees are happy to remind me.

Maybe I think about death too much, focusing on the coming winter, instead of living in the now — when there are still leaves on trees and days when the sun is shining so brightly you could forget there ever was a February at all.

But somehow it makes the now sweeter, for me and maybe for others, to know we only have a short time to absorb fall's beauty.

I remember an autumn years ago, when my husband and I were in the nadir of our struggle to have children, when I was driving in my car after one of my miscarriages. Hormones surging through me, I looked at the trees, as empty and barren as I felt inside, and I could not help but cry. There was death on the trees and death inside me and it felt inescapable. It was inescapable.

Then, from some strange well of hope, a tiny voice reminded me:

They'll be back. The leaves will come back.

And somehow, that cheered me, then and now.

For, yes, autumn is temporary, but so is winter.

Death is there, always threatening, but like all things, death ends. We're not to know what comes next, whether it's heaven or reincarnation or an absorption into the universe's energy, but if it's anything like life, it will be beautiful, as beautiful as a perfect autumn day.

And there we'll all meet, together, at the crossroads.

Don't Listen to Your Inner Hater: It's Not About You Anyway

October 8, 2022

It has come to my attention that I am not universally beloved.

I know, I know. Weird, right?

But, like every person who has ever publicly expressed an opinion, I have gotten hate mail.

I imagine my professional ancestor, a Neanderthal inscribing tablets with his opinions on the stone-tipped arrow shortage, and I bet he got a few rocks lobbed into his cave with the words "you dumb" chipped into them.

Now, my hate mail is nothing serious: No death threats or death wishes or even vague suggestions that I should meet with any form of harm or distress. That I would take seriously, particularly in this quite literally insane political climate in which profiteers leverage fear to motivate the weak-minded.

What I get in my email inbox is more your garden-variety "you're ruining the country" type stuff. Mild and eminently bearable.

Back when I first started writing columns, though, for my college paper, even those tame insults would have gotten under my skin.

Criticisms used to send me into a spiral and each one would

discombobulate me for days, weeks, sometimes even months. In fact, I still remember one such email from the head of the campus recreational center in which she said my column defending an anti-abortion colleague "sucked."

The writer was, in the parlance of today's youth, one of my haters.

Later in life, I've come to realize that I'm not Tom Hanks: Not everyone is going to like me.

Actually, there's probably someone out there who hates Tom Hanks, too.

"Ugh, I'm so sick of hearing how great Tom Hanks is," the person mutters to themselves over their bran flakes or soft-boiled eggs or whatever it is haters eat for breakfast. "So nice, such a good actor, blah blah blah."

If even Tom Hanks can't escape the haters, what hope do I have?

Usually, I respond with a "thanks for reading!" Rarely, I'll defend myself or argue the point, if I have the time and feel like the other person is reasonable. Usually, though, those words are wasted. And the email often really isn't about me. The writers are sad or tired or lonely or angry, and I'm a convenient outlet.

Instead, I clear out the inbox.

I delete and move on.

Plus, the most effective hater isn't sending me all-caps emails. She lives inside my brain.

My inner hater loves to point out every mistake I make, no matter how small. And she sees all of them. (There's a typo in that! Your hair looks crappy! What an unhealthy lunch choice!)

She also has another advantage over strangers lobbing insult-bombs from the internet: I listen to her. Whereas I have no problem dismissing the volleys of those who don't know me, who don't care about me and who, frankly, sometimes don't appear to have even read or understood my writing, the inner hater gets my full attention.

I suspect we all have inner haters.

Even the most confident can have their defensive armor

melted by a self-critique.

As I've gotten older, I've gotten better about countering my inner hater's claims, but she still gets her licks in.

Lately, though, I'm treating my inner hater like an outer one.

It helps to first understand her: The hatred isn't about me. It's about her. She's feeling sad or tired or lonely or angry, and I'm a convenient outlet.

When all is functioning as I'd like and I'm feeling particularly immune to my inner hater, there's one thing I can do: Delete and move on.

Because, ultimately, there's no escaping haters. All you can do is defy their attempts to make you hate yourself.

Haters gonna hate. That's their job.

Our job?

Clear out the inbox.

Endless Fertility Is Not in the Cards for Everyone

October 22, 2022

Like Hilary Swank, you, too, can have your first baby at 48 years old. I just hope you don't bank on it.

After Swank recently announced she was expecting twins, the website Jezebel posted about celebrities who had babies later in life. I worked my way through the article, shocked, as the writer confidently proclaimed Swank's parenthood was proof that "pregnancy can happen on our own timelines."

This isn't the first time a celebrity pregnancy has been used to prop up the false but increasingly common idea that fertility is permanent.

And as someone who underwent fertility treatments in my 30s, I worry that posts like these give regular women a false confidence in their ability to have kids whenever they want. When the rich and famous get pregnant later and later, as Janet Jackson did when she was 50, us regular, non-Janet-Jackson-types might think our path to parenthood can be just as delayed.

The Jezebel post argues it's annoying to have to think about freezing your eggs at 21 years old. I'm sure it is. But you know something else that's annoying? Giving yourself so many hormone injections that you need two different sharps containers for the upstairs and downstairs in your house.

The writer also says that freezing eggs is unfairly expensive, which is unquestionably true. Some other things that are unfairly expensive: IVF, donor eggs, surrogates, adoption lawyers and twins.

I hope, though, that most women will see past the Instagram posts and won't look to millionaires with access to the world's finest fertility treatments to determine whether they will be able to have children whenever they want.

I was young for fertility issues, which often start intensifying after age 35. Nevertheless, it took my husband and I six years to have our first child.

The pregnancy was tough, not just because I was on the cusp of 40 but also because of complications, which can increase both with age and the use of fertility treatments — though it's not clear whether those are the cause or merely a correlation.

Being a parent to young children in your 40s (to say nothing of your 50s) also can be phenomenally difficult, both physically and emotionally.

Do I regret waiting to have children? No. My kids are here and they're wonderful, and I don't know what would have happened if I'd started trying earlier.

Nor do I believe women should be forbidden birth control or abortion. We all should be the authors of our own destiny.

I do, however, wish that as a young woman, I'd had a better understanding of the risks of waiting.

I wish that I would have known that I was risking a chance to have a child without medical treatment, to have a child who shares my or my husband's genes, to carry a pregnancy, to have a child at all.

There are some who will make the same decision either way. They're as happy to adopt or live child-free as they are to carry a child related to them — and thank goodness for that.

And those who want to be parents but don't have a partner or money must make a difficult decision. Would they rather compromise their present — parenting without help or a financial cushion — or compromise their future — one in which they may not share a biological connection with their child or be able to be a parent at all?

And all of that is no guarantee that you can have children at all, no matter what age you start trying.

These aren't easy questions, and they're not fair. But they are, in a sense, just the first of the long series of difficult, unfair questions that parents must answer.

Biology — life itself, even — can be demanding, bizarre and cruel, and that's true no matter who you are. Even if you're Hilary Swank.

'Never Forget' Means First Learning What To Remember

December 17, 2022

At night, after the children are in bed, as I settle down for the evening, I put something horrible on TV.

I fold clothes or brush my teeth to stories of dictators, murderers and mysteries — anything to remind me that no matter how stressful my life gets, it could be a lot worse.

Lately, it's been documentaries about Nazis, the party's rise to power and World War II.

The other night, my husband came in and caught sight of the show I was watching.

"Not World War II again," he said with a groan. "Hitler was evil. What's left to say?"

I laughed. Agreed, the topic has been covered ad nauseam in movies, TV and books. Nazis have become cartoonish bad guys, the ultimate shortcut to villainy. What's left, indeed?

"It's about the Beer Hall Putsch," I explained, the failed coup that Hitler tried in 1923, long before he came to power.

The "putsch," which means "coup" in German, is fascinating for many reasons, but I was mostly struck by its stupidity.

The attempted coup d'etat was drunken and disorganized, hastily conceived and poorly planned. Hitler's men kidnapped but soon released government officials after extracting a promise of fealty to Hitler and his mission. It never occurred to the morons that the men might have been lying to get away with their lives.

"It makes me think of Jan. 6," I told my husband, and the way history has been rewritten to cast the Capitol rioters as harmless idiots.

No one could be that stupid while also being dangerous, the argument seems to go. Jan. 6 was merely a rowdy romp through the halls of Congress that got a little bit out of hand.

We don't know if there was a future Adolf Hitler in the crowds on Jan. 6, 2021. It took more than a decade after the putsch for Hitler to come to power in Germany. In between, he served a short prison term for his part in the coup.

But in attendance on Jan. 6 was Nick Fuentes, a troll who's made a career out of hatred. He has sniggered and joked on his show, doubting the Holocaust's death totals, and casually tossing around racial slurs and antisemitism. Despite that, Fuentes isn't socially isolated and turns up in the wackiest of places, at dinner with Trump at Mar-a-Lago and shaking hands on stage with Rep. Marjorie Taylor Greene.

Now, Fuentes has slyly skirted the line between virulently bigotry and advocating genocide, and Trump and Greene both tried (a little) to distance themselves from him. But it's important to remember, and history reminds us, that things don't usually start out clear-cut. Like a tumbling rock that turns into an avalanche, hatred becomes bolder over time. It shows its true face only after repeat exposure has inured us to it.

We roll our eyes and mumble "that guy's crazy" when Kanye West says "I like Hitler" in an interview with Alex Jones. But West wasn't kicked off the show or forbidden from returning. He's been received, mostly politely, by some in politics, including Fuentes. One prominent conservative, Milo Yiannopoulos, was even connected with West's presidential campaign until they fired him.

So, though it may be true that Nazis aren't new, neither are they particularly old. You'll have to pardon me for thinking these books and documentaries have more to teach me.

For though I'm not convinced we're on a highway toward World War II, it helps to know the route.

Call me alarmist if you like. I don't mind.

Though history may not be repeating itself yet, it may, one day. And if I want to never forget, the first step is learning what to remember.

I'm Off the Train to Cool Town, and I Love It

January 14, 2023

I was at dinner a few weeks ago when the cold hand of approaching death smacked me in the face.

The blow came as I looked at a picture of my husband's friend, a guy I'd last seen 20 years ago.

"He looks so … old," I thought.

Then, a horrifying addendum popped into my brain.

Do I look old, too?

I laughed nervously and glanced at a nearby mirror. The woman who looked back had gray hair and a body that no longer can be mistaken for that of a 22-year-old.

But old? No way.

I admit, having young children doesn't help. Compared to them, I'm ancient, born in a time before cellphones and YouTube.

I remember watching a network TV show with my kids when suddenly one of them gave me a strange look.

"Why did the show stop?" he asked incredulously, having only watched shows on streaming services like Netflix, a seamless experience without interruption. "What's this?"

"That's a commercial," I said, realizing that he had never seen one before, and I felt as old then as an abandoned Cabbage Patch doll, as old as a dried-up bottle of CK One.

Yes, there are plenty of people older than me — to most

members of Congress, I probably seem as fresh-faced as one of Leonardo DiCaprio's girlfriends. But I'm still rapidly approaching the time when I'll demand my kids get in here and help me figure out the remote.

One day soon I'll be old enough that I'll look at the lineup for a music festival, a Lollapalooza or a Coachella or whatever excuse young adults are using to drink too much and engage in ill-advised copulation, and I won't recognize a single performer's name. They'll just be long lists of bands like Doctor Peppercorn and the Cheshire Lightnings, meaningless nonsense.

I'm not far away from that now. I already avoid music venues unless there's a solid chance of being able to sit down.

I've always said that being cool is like riding a train. You're watching the scenery go by, the hip music and movies and fashion, and you're participating in coolness. You still occasionally pick up a new band and you'll buy the "it" fashion items like crop tops or mom jeans. You refer to cool things as "based" and spend $200 to dye your hair from brown to gray.

You're with it, you're moving, you're motoring right along.

Eventually, though, you must pick a stop. You must get off the train.

Doing otherwise is just too exhausting. There are too many things to do as an adult and the last thing you have time for is combing TikTok looking for the latest trends in AI DJs.

So, you'll exit the train, maybe accidentally, maybe a bit wistfully, maybe intentionally and joyfully. Your hair will start looking dated and they'll start playing your music on the "classic rock" radio station.

You're officially uncool, forever, unless your clothes accidentally come back into style.

You're off the train.

Maybe even using a "train" analogy dates me. I should use Uber or electric skateboards or exploding Teslas.

But you get the point. One day you're with it, the next day you're acid-washed jeans and mall bangs. Or maybe those are back in style. I have no clue. Because I got off the train years ago.

And that's fine, because the alternative isn't great. It's tough to be young forever, and I don't have the energy I once had.

There's something encouraging about knowing where you belong, telling someone through your clothes and hairstyle and music where you came from.

Getting older isn't that bad.

Honestly, it's only looking at the pictures that stinks.

Forgive Others — And Yourself — For the Small Mistakes With Big Consequences

February 4, 2023

  I had surgery on my knee recently, the second in a series of operations to correct a problem with my ACL, the problem being that I don't have one.

  I first injured my knee years ago — many, many years ago — at a house party. For a reason that completely eludes me now, I was trying to stop a fight between two guys who I later learned had been drinking for the better part of the day.

  I was, you may have guessed, unsuccessful at stopping the fray, and when Dude A rushed for Dude B, I got pushed aside. Something popped and I felt searing pain. Once my guy friends realized I was hurt, I then had to talk them out of fighting the fighters. It was kind of a mess, and ever since then, my knee has been, too.

  Now, I didn't know the combatants all those years ago. I'm not even sure I knew the person whose house it was. I had no real reason to be invested in the outcome of their fight or in preventing it in the first place. It was just one of those things you do when you're 19, when you think you have a silver tongue and can do anything.

  "I'll handle this," I might have said to myself before walking between the two guys.

For the lack of forethought involved in the decision, it's amazing the impact it's had on me over the years.

The injury has been equal parts troublesome and painful, and it's been plenty of work for my husband and extended family, who pick up the slack when I can't walk or drive.

It's gotten me thinking, though, about the decisions we make, decisions lightly conceived but that weigh heavily on our futures, and how hard it can be to forgive others — and ourselves — for not foreseeing the consequences.

Some, certainly, are more forgiving, or become so as they age. They watch, with empathy, as others choose poorly. They know that we often see the choice as minor, not knowing it's shifting the path of our lives.

A boy I knew in high school once got into a car with a friend we heard had been drinking. Near his house, they crashed into a tree. The friend was fine, but the boy suffered a traumatic brain injury, one that changed him completely.

When I drove by the tree later, I couldn't believe how small it was. Little more than a sapling, it nevertheless had altered everything.

Was it fair, that he should be punished so harshly for a mistake made by so many?

It's a rare person who manages to make it through life sidestepping every slip, outrunning every error, bypassing every blunder. Often, we don't even realize at the time that we're making a bad decision.

Yet our empathy for the errant has its limits. We often draw conclusions, assume an underlying evil that doesn't exist.

We punish them — and ourselves — as if it were easy to divine in advance how our lives would turn out, when something will be deadly and when it will just be a bit of fun.

I've punished myself plenty for my peacekeeping mission those years ago. I've told myself I was arrogant and reckless.

But blame can't change the past. And whatever impulse I had at the time was one born of my personality, my drive to create contentment and prevent hostility. I'm the kind of person who would do what I did, and I didn't make myself that way.

Maybe realizing that can help me forgive myself, as well as others who make similar small mistakes with big consequences.

One thing's for certain: I'll be lousy with opportunities to consider it, lying in bed, recovering. I'll have plenty of free time, and finding grace isn't a bad way to spend it.

'The Now': All We'll Ever Have, and All We Can Ever Enjoy

June 10, 2023

A family member underwent some health problems recently, and when I asked what I could do to help, the answer was "not much."

The only request was that I offer occasional reminders to stay in the moment, to try not to worry about that which cannot be controlled.

It's important work. But, how? How can we live in the present when everything around us — from the news about wildfire smoke polluting the air to the stress of a personal health crisis — tries so hard to pull us into the past or the future?

Often, the more you need to live in "The Now," the more difficult it can be to find.

But the path, in my experience, comes with what's commonly called "mindfulness" — the action of consciously experiencing the present.

First let's agree that there's a big-M "Mindfulness" and a small-M "mindfulness." The former is the kind of meditative activity so popular with therapists, religions and even, lately, academia. My son even gets instruction in big-M Mindfulness in elementary school — deep breathing, focusing on his body — and though that's wonderful, it's small-M mindfulness — finding the elusive "Now" — that's been more effective for me.

When I set out to remember the times it has helped me, I immediately think of my pregnancy with my oldest son.

It was my third pregnancy, the previous two having ended in miscarriage, and from the start, it was a troubled one. I bled, nonstop, more than I thought any pregnant woman could, and I went through months of bed rest — giving me plenty of time to worry about what had already gone wrong and fret about what was to come.

I tried to stop but could not help thinking that I was simply waiting for the other shoe to drop, for the inevitable third miscarriage to come. I had been trying to get pregnant for years, and though there were many terrible steps on that journey, nothing I went through compared to the grief of a miscarriage — the end of hope.

So, during my third pregnancy, out of desperation, I began to pray to my long-dead grandmother — she who had loved me best and most fiercely of all.

I started and ended each day talking to her, and I fell into the habit of beginning our conversations by thanking her for another day of pregnancy. Sometimes, when things seemed particularly grim, I would send her a silent thanks for another minute, another second with a baby inside me.

"Right now, this very second, I am pregnant, and for that, I am grateful," I would think, and it brought me into the present like nothing else.

That's all I had to celebrate — all any of us have to celebrate: The Right Now.

Because everything's going to be OK until the moment that it isn't. There will be loss at the end, and this minute, this second, this instant is all that stands between us and that loss.

As my son has gotten older, he's been joined in our family by a younger brother. I've never felt their lives as imperiled as in the months before my oldest was born. But there have been worries and illnesses, and when I remember to, I deal with my fears the same way I did back then.

"Thank you for another day," I say to my grandmother, at night, when I'm tempted to look into the future or ruminate on the past.

It reminds me that "The Now" is all I have.

I'm not the Dalai Lama, though, and my skillfulness at finding the present changes from day to day. Often, I fail.

The good news, though, is that there's always another present, another "Now." It's here, always, in front of me.

"The Now" awaits me, forever. It awaits us all.

And we always have a new opportunity to claim it.

Greek to Me

Misery Can Make Magic, at Least Where Summers Are Concerned

July 6, 2020

Smack-dab in the middle of a stretch of 90-degree weather, our air conditioning system broke.

Opening the windows did nothing to help. The air outside was dead, heavy and windless.

As our kids dozed fitfully but pants-free, my husband and I lugged out box and desk fans, arranged them for maximum air flow. I propped up a couple of ice packs and draped a wet sheet over them, fantasizing in my heat-induced delirium that the fan blowing over the contraption would serve as a kind of Rube Goldberg air conditioner.

My husband hollered up from the basement that he was trying a "workaround" with the heat sensor.

After we both abandoned our efforts for the night, we sat in the sauna-like living room and stared at each other in resignation.

"It's OK," he said. "We didn't have air conditioning growing up. It stunk but we were fine."

I thought, then, of a summer I spent in Greece, decades ago, the hottest I've ever had.

My parents had put my brother and I on a plane alone to visit our grandparents in the tiny mountain village where they lived.

Our time was both unstructured and wholly unsupervised.

We ran with a pack of village kids sometimes. Other times, my brother and I would wander off together or alone, clambering up into the mountains like goats.

Once, a wizened yia-yia with a black-and-yellow scarf tied tightly around her head dropped a fat bag of cherries into my lap as I played by a stream. She rode off on her donkey, and my brother and I sat, eating cherries until our fingers and mouths turned red from the juice.

We often played foosball in the village coffee shop, horrifying both my grandfather, who was scandalized by my fraternizing with boys, and my grandmother, who had to grind out on a washboard our clothes' grease stains from the foosball table's oiled rods.

But the summer's headiest magic came in the sweltering days we spent at our grandparents' beach shack.

My grandfather drove my brother, two of my cousins and me to the beach house, and left us there, alone. I was about 13, my brother roughly 10. Our cousins were similar ages. Maybe we were only adult-free for a few days, but in my child brain, the sojourn stretched out for glorious weeks.

The shack we stayed in was no more than a three-room concrete building on blocks. A bucket sat outside the outhouse at the back. A tin container held water to drink and wash ourselves with.

My grandfather came once or twice a day to drop off fresh water and cook us food. I remember no meal as satisfying as the crisp fried potatoes, feta cheese and salad he would dole out on plastic plates.

Each day, we found a new adventure. We wandered down the beach and made 20-foot-long sandcastles, took spears out to "hunt" for sea urchins and invented a marching song set to "The Battle Hymn of the Republic."

Then, one day, the desert wind swept in.

Other kids staying further down the beach told us that it was an African wind, blowing up over the Mediterranean Sea from Egypt and Libya.

"It comes sometimes," a girl told me, shaking her head in

warning.

I've never felt anything as parched, as dry as that wind. It did not refresh, instead pulling moisture from the air and your skin as it wafted past. You could get some relief in the ocean, but the instant you left the water, the wind was like a hair dryer on your skin.

That first night, we rolled over and over in the cots in the beach house, trying to get comfortable. Outside, we could hear music and kids laughing. My brother, my cousins and I went outside.

"We're sleeping on the beach!" the kids told us, and we set up our towels alongside theirs. A bonfire crackled a little bit away and in the flickering light, teenagers and kids danced to Greek music on a boombox.

The other kids knew my brother and I were Americans but knew nothing about American culture other than "break-dancing" and "Michael Jordan."

"Break-dance!" one of the kids ordered me, and I awkwardly did The Robot to oohs and aahs from those watching. I'm not sure what time we fell asleep, how we even did, considering the heat.

The next day, the arid wind was gone, and with it some of the uncanny feel of the night before.

As an adult, I realize that it was days like those, strange and uncomfortable, that would become the gems of my childhood memories.

The air-conditioner days? Those are too common, stack up by the thousands like tissue paper, so thin you can barely see them.

When the sweaty days, full of ugly, hot winds, blow in, maybe we shouldn't try to rush through them. Maybe those are the days that count. I don't have much choice with our air conditioner taking a paid vacation right now, but anyway, I suppose that's what I'll choose to believe.

(c) 2023 Pioneer Press. All rights reserved. Distributed by Tribune Content Agency, LLC

The Greek 'No,' and the Long Tendrils of Old Evils

January 8, 2022

My grandmother once told me the story of the Greek "no."

Greeks, you may or may not know, mime the word "no" differently. Instead of moving their heads side to side in a shake, they lift their chins imperiously, raising their eyebrows, in a motion both striking and confusing in its similarity to the nod that means "yes" in almost every other language.

My Yia-Yia, her fierce eyes shining under the canopy of a yellow and black silk headscarf, explained it to me thusly:

"During the occupation" — a mild way of putting hundreds of years of Ottoman rule over Greece — "the Turks held their curved swords underneath the Greeks' chins ... "

Here, she would demonstrate with a finger to her throat.

"And they asked, 'Will you swear to Allah?' If the Greeks shook their head 'no' ... "

Again, she would mime, showing the sword-finger's deadly path across her neck.

"Instead," she explained, "they said 'no' like this."

Then, she would click her tongue in disgust, raising her eyebrows and chin as high as they could go, creating a dramatic and perfect Greek "no."

"It's true," she told me, with finality.

I did not as a child, nor ever after, respond with my current belief, that the story seems highly unlikely to have even the slightest basis in truth.

I did not explain that the Ottoman Empire didn't, historically, much care for forced conversions, nor did I point out that if they had, when the Greeks said "no," they probably were headed for a beheading no matter which way they moved their heads to say it.

I did not express my uneducated guess that the reason for the divergence from custom was far more likely explained by the Greek contrarian spirit. I mean, come on, we *spit* at cute babies.

I did not say any of those things because I understood then, as I do now, that the Turks, in the minds of my grandmother and those of her generation, were something more than real.

The Turks were, in their minds and in their memories, both actual oppressors and cartoonish boogeymen. They were a true evil stretched out to fantastical proportions.

Some of my grandmother's older relatives knew of or had themselves been subjected by Turks to forced migrations, military conscriptions, ill-treatment and starvation in Anatolia. My great-grandfather, her husband's father, had been exiled from Turkey in the mass exchange of Christians and Muslims that took place in 1923. He almost certainly had heard of or even seen for himself the massacres of Pontic Greeks and Armenians that had taken place there.

Therefore, I could not and do not blame my grandmother for seeing Turks behind every tree, like marauding intruders, for alternately blaming them for and crediting them with creating almost every aspect of the Greek experience.

For great sins, and those who committed them, can live on.

We cannot, sometimes, escape these villains, even when they present to us no current threat, even after they're gone, even when their bones and the bones of all those they hurt have been turned to dust.

It does no good to deny them, to pretend as if the scars

weren't real, to tell ourselves that it was so, so long ago. Because perhaps, probably, clearly, it hasn't been long enough.

That's the only way out, after all. Like water over a pebble, only time can remove the sharp edges from sin.

One day, we won't remember what our father's father's father said, the stories they told of the hunger and the deprivation and the suffering. We won't remember the cruelty.

Only then — when it has been ages and years directly proportional to the evil and the length of time for which it was perpetrated — well, then, maybe it will be enough.

Maybe, then, we will forget.

The Oily Reason I'm Worried About Flying

June 24, 2022

  I got a haircut recently, and as the stylist snipped, she asked a question. Her ex-husband had protested when she wanted to put their girls on a plane, solo, to visit family a couple of hours away.

  "Did you ever fly alone as a kid?"

  Dear Reader, I laughed then — a hearty guffaw.

  For, you see, the list of things I did alone as a child was long and included much more than flying.

  I grew up before the advent of dawn-to-dusk supervision, so my brothers and I were sometimes pushed onto a plane to Greece to spend three months in the care of our grandparents, sans parents.

  My younger brother remembers one trip where his connecting flight was delayed and he spent a night in New York, alone, which sounds like the plot of "Home Alone 2" but actually was just the life of a kid in the 1980s.

  My grandfather picked us up at the Athens airport and drove us to their tiny village, and woe betide us if we'd forgotten our Greek in the preceding year. My grandfather spoke no English, though my grandmother eventually learned a few words after hearing my brother and I screech "Shut up!" and "Stop it!"

at each other enough times.

In the village, we roamed free, traipsing off into the mountains or running to the coffee shop to play foosball with other feral children.

All the villagers knew whose kids we were, and they'd report back when necessary. I don't remember anyone ever being worried we might get hurt, but they sure did tattle on us.

My little brother and I happened upon a stream one year, and we instantly became a mini Army Corps of Engineers, tidying up and removing pebbles blocking its flow. We returned the next day and industriously re-shoveled the pebbles, which had mysteriously reappeared.

After the third day, a farmer appeared at my grandparents' house, yelling through the door to my grandmother.

"Your grandkids are flooding my garden!" he shouted, and that was the moment I learned about natural irrigation systems.

Another year, when I was 13 and my younger brother 10, my grandparents drove us a half-hour away to a beach shack and left us there, unsupervised for a week, with two similar-aged cousins.

There was no electricity or running water at the shack, which had two bedrooms, a small kitchen and an outhouse that we flushed with a bucket of seawater. We checked our shoes and clothes for scorpions, which wouldn't strike unless you touched them.

My grandfather stopped by once a day to cook us a meal — fried potatoes, feta cheese and salad, usually — and drop off fresh water for drinking and washing our hair.

During the day, we swam, fished with tri-tipped spears and wandered down to a lonely bay where waves crashed over giant rocks shaped like dominoes.

At night, we blew out the oil lamps and curled our sun-burned bodies onto thin cots to sleep.

It was one of the best times of my childhood, when my mind and body were as free to soar as I liked.

After I'd recounted this, the hairstylist asked another

question.

"Would you let your kids do that?"

I laughed again.

My husband and I would get arrested if we did (perhaps rightfully so), but kids in 2023 also haven't been prepared for such a thorough entrance into the world. They've always been surrounded by adults' eyes, and they're not ready to be so alone, so unseen.

We talked, then, about how freedom has risks but also its rewards.

We've made trade-offs for safety, but we wondered what children — and adults — have lost in the exchange.

Fewer of us fall into wells and out of trees. Fewer of us drown.

But, we admitted, fewer of us swim. Fewer of us climb.

Fewer of us soar.

Banish the Chaos — At Least for a Little While

July 16, 2022

In Greece, members of parliament come from dozens of political parties, varying on the spectrum from neo-fascists with logos eerily evocative of swastikas to Putin-sympathetic communists.

You might call it chaotic, with some seats occupied by fringe extremists and parties forced to align with those with whom they share only a loose approximation of agreement.

It has always been thus in Greece, though, where political chaos is a hallmark.

After all, it was the Classical Greeks who created ostracism, an annual vote taken on whether to banish a person from the city for 10 years. Ostracism could be dispensed for any reason — even pure spite.

In one anecdote from Plutarch, a man says he wishes to ostracize Aristides the Just simply because he's sick of hearing him lauded.

Now, Donald Trump is no one's idea of just, but I'm finding myself longing for the chaos of ostracism lately, with the former president announcing he's going to run again in 2024.

I don't know if I can take another two years of mean-spirited pageantry and the further destruction of what remains of our national dignity. I don't know if I can take another assault on a free and fair election, one in which it is certain that Trump will declare victory, no matter the results.

I suppose it's not even so much Trump's running but his inescapable presence that bothers me.

Yes, it's disturbing that so many of my fellow countrymen live in the kind of cruel world Trump embodies, one in which ethics are for suckers, the weak are fodder for mockery and women are mere hunks of meat awaiting consumption.

But Trump's appeal reminds me of a poem by Greek poet Yannis Ritsos, "Smoked Earthen Pot," in which he corresponds with a fellow poet:

My brother sometime ago we were very proud
because we weren't confident at all
We said big words
we placed many gold stripe on the arm of our verse
a tall crown waved on the forehead of our song
we were noisy — we were afraid and for this we were noisy
covering our fear with our voices
we pounded our heels on the sidewalk
long strides reverberating
like those in parades with empty cannons

Trumpian chest-thumping comes from a place of fear, clearly, but the fact of his constant, irritating presence in our discourse remains.

I'm comforted, a bit, by the knowledge that it was not so long ago that Trump lost a presidential election, handily, to the office's current occupier. Enough voters saw through Trump's bluster to the dangerously insecure man inside.

But there's always danger when you talk about Trump, a man who forcefully pushed the narrative — one now commonly (if not privately) accepted as fact by almost the entire GOP — that he won the last election, despite mountains of evidence to the contrary.

For yes, the cannons are now empty, but there's always the danger that, one day, he will fill them, as he did on Jan. 6, 2021, using the rage and fear of his followers as ammunition.

And although the cosplaying stupidity of Jan. 6 may seem little threat now, the boundaries of acceptable presidential behavior were moved that day somewhere to the right of "utter lawlessness."

So, I find myself thinking of the Classical Greeks, enviously, as people who very well may have been onto something with that whole ostracism thing.

I mean, if we're going to have the chaos, I'd like to at least have a way of getting a break from it.

The only problem is, I'm not sure 10 years will be long enough. Can we make it an even 20?

For the Perfect Summer Vacation, Just Add Time

August 13, 2022

For children, vacations pass in a haze of pleasantness.

Distance and inconvenience disappear into a fog of naps, snacks and entertainment, and they never have to remember to check the plane's seatback pocket. They don't see a check at a restaurant, examine the line items on a hotel bill or set an alarm to make an early flight.

I, however, am no longer a child.

When we adults go on vacation, as our family did recently to Greece, it is a tangle of mad dashes to ferry boats, flat tires at the tops of mountains and kids who don't understand why there's never any maple syrup for Greek pancakes.

While my children enjoyed the salty breeze in a seaside cafe, I wandered around on an unfamiliar island in 90-degree heat begging Greek strangers to help me find a vacation rental that might as well have been the lost city of Atlantis for as much good as the GPS directions did.

And all this stress was with the *help* of modern conveniences. Who knows how our parents did it in the days when you had to trace your route on giant, impossible-to-re-fold maps and manage dinners using nothing more diverting than crayons and a paper placemat.

It puts into perspective the family trips of our youth, where our parents dragged us over oceans on planes, in cars for endless hours and to far-flung beaches without the benefit of Google Maps, Netflix and convenience stores at every corner, stocked with every food and beverage known to man.

I wondered what my parents' memories of those trips were, what they thought about the time my kid brother threw up in the van on the way up the Smoky Mountains or the long car ride when my other brother and I lobbed open packets of honey into the front seat one night when we were bored.

Of course, not everything was harder back then. We took off our seatbelts in the car and curled up on the floor to play, and airplanes weren't the mobile jail cells they are now. The seats certainly weren't so tiny and close together that reclining caused you to risk violence from angry passengers behind you.

I thought about all of this in Greece as I watched my children snooze in the car on the way back from the beach. While they slept, my husband drove twisty mountain passes and I balanced my phone on my knee so I could simultaneously watch the directions and look outside to avoid getting carsick.

How sweetly slumberous they looked, tanned but not sunburned and freshly changed out of their wet swimsuits. They trusted that we would get them to their destination safely, trusted that when they awoke, they would be fed and when they were bored, plied with video games and coloring books.

Their memories of our vacation would be smoother than ours, the wrinkles ironed out by time and a child's mind.

Which, I decided ultimately, was fine.

For though in some ways, the trip was for them, in other, more important ways, it was not.

It was so that my husband and I might eventually shake our heads in amazement at how we survived and laugh at what wasn't funny, at the time.

Our children's memories of the weeks would be hazy, incomplete and, yes, perfect, but ours would be shockingly clear.

And though those experiences would not be what he and I

would have ordered up while planning the trip, they would be, to our minds, just as wonderful — if not more so — than whatever idealized vacation we could have dreamed up.

And, therefore, it would be worth it. Worth the money, worth the misery, worth the time.

The trip would be, in its own fashion and judged by all the metrics that matter, perfect.

Treasure Hunting on Vacation

August 20, 2022

I came home from Greece with a bag full of rocks.

I brought back more than I should have, but considering the giant pile I'd amassed before we left, far fewer than I wanted.

I measured the time we were there by my rock collection, which grew, slowly some days and rapidly others.

When my kids grew tired of the beach, or when they seemed to be angling for me to hand over my phone so they could play games or watch videos, I'd ask them to come hunt for rocks.

Sometimes, we searched for sea glass to give to their grandmother.

"Which color is the most rare?" my son asked and, with an insistence common in youthful questioning, would not allow me to demur.

He wanted me to look up the definitive answer on my phone, but I took the old-fashioned route of supreme parental confidence.

"Probably purple," I said, thinking that I hadn't seen many purple glass bottles in my days.

On other hunts, I asked the kids to find me a particular kind of stone — "as white and smooth as an egg," I once requested.

They compared the white rocks as they found them,

seeking the one that would match my description the best.

Which was the smoothest? The most egg-like in shape? The most opaque?

And then there were the rocks we added to the collection because of their uniqueness. My son chose one because it looked like a heart. Another because it reminded him of Pac-Man. Our younger son picked one that was just the right shade of blue, his favorite color.

Some days we left the beach with bags and buckets heavy with rocks, ones they and I couldn't bear to leave behind.

Looking for the stones, I was reminded of similar searches when I was a child, on some of the same beaches I was now combing as an adult.

I remember finding pebbles — some a shocking green, others swirled with pink and white — and being sad to see them once they were out of the water, their colors faded to variants of dull gray.

I tried rubbing them with olive oil to see if that would return their vibrancy, but it somehow didn't work. They were different once removed from the salty sea.

It was a challenge to determine which rocks I'd bring back from our vacation. I reluctantly put some of them back, in garden beds full of other rocks and back on the pebbled shore, but I would have brought them all if I could.

The remainder I divvied up. Some for both of my sons, some for me, most of the sea glass to their grandmother. (We saved one special piece for each of us.)

The boys' rocks went into their treasure chest, cigar boxes that hold precious trinkets like seashells, feathers and particularly beautiful cupcake toppers.

Mine, about a dozen of the smallest and smoothest of our selection, now sit on my desk. They're waiting for just the right dish to hold them, a dish that's pretty but not so pretty that it distracts.

I touch them often, picking them up to feel their smoothness, discovering new cracks and spots that I'd missed before.

They're mostly whites, pastel grays and pinks, but there's one that stands out. It looks like a large jellybean, sheer white speckled with brick red. When we first found it, the 4-year-old popped it in his mouth. He couldn't help himself.

"I wanted to see how it tasted," he said.

It does look delicious.

I tell myself it's silly to think these are rare and valuable gems, but I can't stop the thought from popping up.

They're just pebbles, I say.

Their value, I'm certain, is only in my mind.

But that's valuable enough.

The Ancient Greek Argument Against the Death Penalty

October 15, 2022

If someone deserves to die, should we kill them?

That's what I asked myself recently, as I read the news that the jurors recommended life in prison instead of the death penalty for Nikolas Cruz, the Parkland school killer.

His crimes were unquestionably heinous. He murdered more than a dozen children and teachers and permanently traumatized many others, and he did it in a place that should have been a sanctuary. He was ruthless and premeditated. The suffering he caused is incalculable.

And yet, I find myself agreeing with the jurors.

My opinion may be worse than worthless in this situation, but I can't help but having it. I can't help thinking it: Death should not be compounded by death.

The Ancient Greeks had a term for what happens when you kill someone: miasma. Blood guilt.

They believed miasma infected a killer but also the society in which he lived, and permeated everything and everyone around him. Miasma led to further wrongs and created further suffering — even in innocents. Victims had to avenge it, but their revenge, in turn, just created more miasma.

The belief in miasma was one of the reasons the death

penalty was so rarely enforced in Classical Athens. Often, murderers were allowed to escape, and when they were executed, it was typically in secondhand ways that allowed the executioners to escape full responsibility.

No one killed Socrates, in other words. Socrates killed himself by drinking the hemlock.

And though it's silly to think blood guilt had technicality loopholes, the Ancient Greeks felt they had to do something. They didn't want the blood on their hands, either.

For when we kill someone, it taints us.

It wasn't just the Ancient Greeks who believed that.

It's the reason why, during executions by firing squad, sometimes one or more of the gunmen are given blank or dummy rounds, protecting them from the miasma, from the stain of blood.

But what about the incurably evil? Perhaps killing them is different.

The other day, my son asked me if I hated one of his classmates, a "big meanie" who made a little girl cry.

"No, I feel sorry for him," I said. "Because when you hurt someone, you get a yucky feeling inside."

"But what if he likes the yucky feeling?" my son asked.

It's a good question. Because some do. They like the yucky feeling and are irretrievably drawn to it, will seek it out — over and over — until and unless they are stopped. And we must stop them.

But people who like the yucky feeling — whether they're evil or simply broken — are alive, and the law should protect their lives, the same as it does yours and mine.

Justice cannot, should not, be about parsing who deserves death. You can't be allowed to murder a deadbeat dad any more than you can be allowed to murder a single mother.

The immorality of the crime is not dependent on the morality of the victim.

That's why it's reprehensible when victims are attacked for not being innocent enough, as if shortcomings or sins make them acceptable targets for crime.

Under the law, everyone's life should be valuable, inherently, for no other reason than that we only have one.

In saving his life, Cruz's defense team seems to have successfully pulled jurors' heartstrings. One fetal alcohol expert testified that, while pregnant with him, Cruz's mother drank more than any other woman he'd heard of in decades of studying the topic.

To me, that's unfortunate but irrelevant to his punishment.

For in determining whether to take his life, we must consider the consequences - but not to him. We must consider the consequences to us.

Though he may deserve to die, we first should ask a more important question:

Do we deserve to be killers?

Oxi Day Reminds Us of the Value of a 'No'

October 29, 2022

There's power in a "no."

Just ask the Greeks, who celebrate the word every year, on Oxi Day, Oct. 28.

It's a day created in honor of the Greeks' most famous "no," the one given to Benito Mussolini's ambassador after he ordered Greek Prime Minister Ioannis Metaxas to let the Italian army occupy Greece.

"No!" Metaxas allegedly responded. (His actual quote was, "Alors, c'est la guerre," meaning, "Then it's war," but that's less pithy, and "No!" better captures the spirit of the thing.)

Two and a half hours after the ultimatum, Italy invaded Greece, coming over the northern border with Albania.

Oxi, or "no," is the motto of the 8th Infantry Division of the Hellenic Army, the first Greek men to battle the Axis forces. The 8th successfully repelled the Italians, making time for the Greek reserves to mobilize.

No.

Hitler would soon come to Italy's aid and, feeling confident, he attacked Crete in what would become a famous battle.

As the Germans parachuted onto the island in May of 1941, the outmanned and out-equipped Greeks refused to quit.

Villagers grabbed cooking knives and pitchforks and attacked the Nazis as they landed. One old man clubbed a German paratrooper to death with his cane.

Though the Greeks lost, the experience humiliated Germany and delayed the invasion of Russia enough that some credit it with aiding the Allied win.

No.

When the Nazi government in occupied Greece began to deport Greek Jews, allegedly to work during the war, the archbishop of Greece, Damaskinos, protested repeatedly and publicly.

The German official in charge ordered the archbishop to stop his efforts, threatening to execute him by firing squad.

Damaskinos' reply was that Greek clergy "are hanged, not shot" and he asked that the Nazis "please respect our traditions." Instead of ceasing his work, the archbishop ordered Greek Orthodox churches to provide fake baptismal certificates for Jews and told Greeks to hide their Jewish neighbors in their homes.

No.

Meanwhile, the chief rabbi of Athens, Elias Barzilai, was working furiously to save the Jewish people in Athens, both the residents and refugees from other countries.

He gathered together the city's Jewish population and told them to flee. He worked with Greek guerrillas to disperse as many Jews as he could to the mountains, and the Jewish men in their ranks joined the Greek rebels in fighting the Nazis.

When Barzilai was ordered to turn over a list of all the Jews in the area, he destroyed the records. Instead, he produced a certificate, given by the German government after an earlier break-in, saying the records had been stolen by burglars.

No.

On April 27, 1941, a man, Konstantinos Koukidis, was the Greek guard assigned to the Acropolis in Athens. When he was ordered to lower the Greek flag and install the Nazi one in its place, legend has it that the man instead wrapped the flag around himself and jumped to his death.

A month later, two teenagers, Manolis Glezos and

Apostolos Santas, climbed up in the dark of night to pull down the Nazi flag.

The perpetrators, then unknown to the Germans, were sentenced to death, but the teens could not be found when no Greeks turned Glezos or Santas over. Instead, the two 19-year-olds joined the resistance and became Greek folk heroes.

No.

As stirring as they may be, these stories aren't stories of victories.

Instead, they're stories of pushing back.

They're stories of obstinance in the face of evil — of deciding what is right and then refusing to be parted from it.

We honor the word "no" on Oxi Day, though more appropriately, we should cherish it always.

For there's power in a "no," and valor in a struggle.

May their memories be eternal.

What's Greek Easter When You Have the Other Kind?

April 15, 2023

The other night, my kids ate corn dogs and feta cheese for dinner.
That might seem odd unless I add that I am, and they therefore also are, Greek.
Growing up, feta was always on our table. It was ever-present, like salt, or napkins. If we ate fried chicken, there was feta. Spaghetti? Feta. Steak? Feta.
My dad was in town recently, and during dinner, he asked me to bring him the feta. When I told him I was almost out, it was like admitting I'd run out of toilet paper.
But we're Greeks. We do things differently. Which is why this Sunday, long after the last tears have been shed over egg hunts, Greeks will be stuffing their kids into fancy outfits and keeping them up past midnight for Greek Easter celebrations.
Orthodox Easter usually comes on a different day from Catholic and Protestant Easter.
Why?
Because we want to be different, and because we never admit that we're wrong.
The Julian calendar, on which Greek Easter is based, was introduced in 46 BCE, and, despite advances in astronomy that led to the more accurate Gregorian calendar, Greeks have stuck to the

old one. We don't want your new-fangled "correct" calendar. Ours works perfectly fine.

But if I'm honest, I admit that it's hard having two Easters, if for no other reason than the challenge of winning over kids who have exposure to both kinds.

It doesn't help that they're usually still riding a sugar high from non-Greek Easter, when they were given so much chocolate they started politely declining it.

By the time Greek Easter rolls around, there's not much to recommend it.

"What do we do on Greek Easter, Mom?"

"We dye eggs, boys."

"Oh! Like, cool colors and glitter and stripes with stickers?"

"No, red. Only red. The color of blood."

"I see."

There's no Greek Easter bunny, so there are no egg hunts. The only sporting event is a vicious competition in which the family takes a bloody egg and slams it up against their neighbor's to see whose cracks, repeating until there's only one winner and everyone else is left crying.

There are, it must be admitted, the traditional Greek Easter treats.

The first is magiritsa — basically, Greek chitlin soup. The first time I saw my grandmother make magiritsa, I asked my dad what it was.

"Lamb intestines," he said, then seeing my horrified look, added, "But don't worry. Yia Yia washes them really well."

After you've choked down a bowl of magiritsa, it's time for dessert: koulourakia and tsoureki.

Koulourakia are cookies. What flavor cookie, you ask, thinking that surely there must be a special Easter spice or addition. Well, no. They're cookie-flavored cookies. A particularly avant-garde recipe might call for orange zest, but otherwise, they're just … cookies. Very, very dry cookies.

Tsoureki, similarly, is bread. Slightly sweet bread, yes, but still … bread. It does have an egg in the middle, though! A red one. For blood.

For kids, there are fancy candles. It's a newish tradition, but

Greek parents now often buy their children giant, rococo candles covered in bunting and bows, swirled with tulle and dotted with fabric flowers. They cost somewhere in the neighborhood of $40, and you know children really appreciate them because after holding them in church for about an hour, the candles are transformed into what is, essentially, very frilly trash.

I can't sell any of that to my kids.

But one day, maybe, they'll get it. Because the real appeal of Greek Easter is to adults.

After days of cooking, you go to church for midnight Mass. Then you come home. You invite over family and friends. You sit and you eat: lamb, pastitsio or moussaka — maybe even koulourakia. (The kids won't touch them, so there'll be plenty left over.) Maybe you drink wine. You talk. You listen to music.

It's glorious.

It's different.

But better than all that, it's Greek.

And *that* they might understand.

Kalo Pasca.

Remembrance of Childhood Illnesses Past

May 13, 2023

    Our house has once more laid low, this time by the dual demons of injury and illness.
    I'm hobbled, recovering from knee surgery, and the boys have been cycling through waxing and waning phases of never-ending coughs. Then, they both got strep, which in some ways is great because we can give them antibiotics and push them out the door to school the next day, and in other ways is terrible because the reason we know it's strep is the puking.
    You see, we have a puker in the house.
    Every time my one boy gets sick, he pukes. Has stomach flu, pukes. Regular flu? Puke. Hand, foot and mouth? Puke. My chief memory of his infancy is of cleaning up vomit. My husband and I had it down to military precision, in which I would yell "TIM!" and he would run into the kids' room holding a spray bottle and paper towels, and I would run in the opposite direction holding out a wailing child like an offering, racing to the bathtub to denude and hose him down.
    And though our other child isn't an expert puker, he certainly does dabble.
    This round of sickness got me thinking about my own childhood illnesses, though, and the barbaric and wonderful treatments we were put through to manage them.

First of all, there were no viral or bacterial causes of disease when I was growing up. According to my Greek grandmother, all illness could be traced to three root causes:
1. Walking outside with wet hair.
2. Walking barefoot on wood or stone floors.
3. Air conditioning.

When I was sick as a child, she'd light an alcohol-soaked cotton ball in a glass jar, then quickly remove it, causing the glass jar to stick to my back. I guess it was supposed to draw out something foul - whatever miasma attacked barefoot kids, maybe?

They called the treatment "vendouzes," though I have since learned that other people call it "cupping," and celebrities like Gwyneth Paltrow pay thousands of dollars to be subjected to it.

My American mother, who was horrified at such Old World quackery, was more in line with the Vicks-and-antibiotics style of 1980s medicine. Things have certainly changed, but I remember when antibiotics were handed out like candy - though come to think of it, even candy isn't handed out like candy anymore.

And when we were sick, there wasn't great joy in staying home from school - mostly because, unless you were partial to soap operas and "The Price Is Right," the TV stunk. Now my sons have hot-and-cold entertainment, video games and Netflix at the tips of their fingers.

I do, however, douse them in Vicks VapoRub.

"Not the spicy cream!" my younger son cries when he spies the little blue jar.

I slather it on them like it's butter and they're a Thanksgiving turkey, wrap them in warm clothes and turn up the humidifier so high you can write ransom notes on the windows.

Periodically, I will demand that they blow their nose. If they balk, I threaten to pull out "The Snot Sucker," a torture instrument from their baby days that literally sucks all the mucus out of their noses. I boast an unblemished record of compliance.

My Greek dad, however, who is his mother's son, will tell me every time the boys are sick that it's solely due to the temperature at which we keep the home.

"The air conditioner," he said solemnly, after I told him our younger boy had pneumonia.

But antibiotics worked on him, and, despite the continued pervasiveness of central air, he recovered fully.

As for me, I don't get many sick days now, but when I do, I'm partial to cherry NyQuil, orange juice and canned chicken noodle soup, heated to a temperature that would make Hades blush.

And you know what?

It works.

At least as well as sticking burning-hot jars to your back does, anyway. And I never, ever go barefoot.

Tales of the Summer Camp From Hell

June 17, 2023

In our house, it's the time of year when kids stop complaining about school and start complaining about summer camp.

"Ugh," my son says as he hops out of the car to go swimming and crafting and playing on playgrounds.

It seems like a sweet gig to me, but maybe that's because when I was a kid, I went to the summer camp from hell.

Now, it was an unusual camp in many ways, chiefly in that it was run, in Greece, by a group of Evangelical Christians. Fully 90% or more of Greece's population is Greek Orthodox, and I'm sure that number was even higher then. Non-Orthodox Christians are *seriously* going against the grain, and I guess they also decided to go against the grain in terms of the fun activities common at summer camps.

Each day at this sleepaway camp, we were awoken at 7 a.m., not by music or trombones but by counselors spraying us with water mixed with perfume. As they did this, they giggled maniacally, effectively destroying any misapprehension that it was intended as anything other than entertainment for the adults running the place.

"Stop!" we'd scream, covering ourselves with sheets. "We're up, we're up!"

The real losers were the kids in the top bunks, which were impossible to quickly escape. The spritzing continued until we could scramble into the bathroom to dress.

Once we had been properly shocked into consciousness, we headed to the cafeteria for breakfast.

Now, I was an American kid, so my breakfast expectations included eggs, bacon, pancakes — at least cereal and milk. Instead, we had just two choices: tea and toast.

I accepted the tea with a look of confusion, for an adult had never before offered me a hot caffeinated beverage. The last thing my parents wanted was to keep me awake.

And lest you get the wrong idea, by "toast," I do not mean thick bread covered in cheese, butter or avocado. It was a meager, penitentiary slice, lightly smeared with margarine and accompanied by a brown jelly of indeterminate fruit origin.

I looked around at the other campers, who didn't seem put off.

"Kids must not eat in Greece," I thought.

Now, as in any good correctional institution, there was a commissary selling chips and candy, but I didn't have money for that. My parents didn't consider the possibility that I would be extorted for nourishment.

Instead, my chief memory of the camp is of sitting in an interminable series of church services, stinking of perfume, with a rumbling stomach, waiting for lunch.

Church was held in a catacomb-dark medieval chapel, the kind I was accustomed to from Greek Orthodox services. But like most Greek Orthodox people, I was also accustomed to exiting that church into the light of day after a reasonable period of time.

There, though, the pastor droned on for hours, and we dozed, heads slumping onto each other's shoulders, only to be periodically shouted awake once he noticed we were out.

Between homilies, we were allowed outside to play, in a field near the chapel.

In that dirt churchyard, I made friends — real friends.

It was a tight, "Shawshank Redemption" bond, and when the two weeks of camp were over, I cried saying goodbye to my cellmates.

"It's over!" we sobbed, clinging to each other, realizing that we'd never cross paths again. But, really, it was for the best. Why on earth would we want to remember summer camp?

When my parents asked how camp was, I shuddered.

"Let's never speak of it again," I said.

In short, my kids will have to forgive me if I'm less than sympathetic to their camp complaints.

Listening to them come home, grousing about how the line at the amusement park for the bumper cars was too long, I'm tempted to give them a taste of *my* summer camp experience.

All I'd need for that craft project is perfume, a spray bottle and a really strange sense of humor.

What Have We Lost in the Exchange for Our Children's Safety?

June 24, 2023

I got a haircut recently, and as the stylist snipped, she asked a question. Her ex-husband had protested when she wanted to put their girls on a plane, solo, to visit family a couple of hours away.

"Did you ever fly alone as a kid?"

Dear Reader, I laughed then — a hearty guffaw.

For, you see, the list of things I did alone as a child was long and included much more than flying.

I grew up before the advent of dawn-to-dusk supervision, so my brothers and I were sometimes pushed onto a plane to Greece to spend three months in the care of our grandparents, sans parents.

My younger brother remembers one trip where his connecting flight was delayed and he spent a night in New York, alone, which sounds like the plot of "Home Alone 2" but actually was just the life of a kid in the 1980s.

My grandfather picked us up at the Athens airport and drove us to their tiny village, and woe betide us if we'd forgotten our Greek in the preceding year. My grandfather spoke no English, though my grandmother eventually learned a few words after hearing my brother and I screech "Shut up!" and "Stop it!"

at each other enough times.

In the village, we roamed free, traipsing off into the mountains or running to the coffee shop to play foosball with other feral children.

All the villagers knew whose kids we were, and they'd report back when necessary. I don't remember anyone ever being worried we might get hurt, but they sure did tattle on us.

My little brother and I happened upon a stream one year, and we instantly became a mini Army Corps of Engineers, tidying up and removing pebbles blocking its flow. We returned the next day and industriously re-shoveled the pebbles, which had mysteriously reappeared.

After the third day, a farmer appeared at my grandparents' house, yelling through the door to my grandmother.

"Your grandkids are flooding my garden!" he shouted, and that was the moment I learned about natural irrigation systems.

Another year, when I was 13 and my younger brother 10, my grandparents drove us a half-hour away to a beach shack and left us there, unsupervised for a week, with two similar-aged cousins.

There was no electricity or running water at the shack, which had two bedrooms, a small kitchen and an outhouse that we flushed with a bucket of seawater. We checked our shoes and clothes for scorpions, which wouldn't strike unless you touched them.

My grandfather stopped by once a day to cook us a meal — fried potatoes, feta cheese and salad, usually — and drop off fresh water for drinking and washing our hair.

During the day, we swam, fished with tri-tipped spears and wandered down to a lonely bay where waves crashed over giant rocks shaped like dominoes.

At night, we blew out the oil lamps and curled our sunburned bodies onto thin cots to sleep.

It was one of the best times of my childhood, when my mind and body were as free to soar as I liked.

After I'd recounted this, the hairstylist asked another

question.

"Would you let your kids do that?"

I laughed again.

My husband and I would get arrested if we did (perhaps rightfully so), but kids in 2023 also haven't been prepared for such a thorough entrance into the world. They've always been surrounded by adults' eyes, and they're not ready to be so alone, so unseen.

We talked, then, about how freedom has risks but also its rewards.

We've made trade-offs for safety, but we wondered what children — and adults — have lost in the exchange.

Fewer of us fall into wells and out of trees. Fewer of us drown.

But, we admitted, fewer of us swim. Fewer of us climb.

Fewer of us soar.

Superstitions May Be Silly, but That Doesn't Mean They're Bad

July 15, 2023

The other day, my son asked me why the number 13 is unlucky.

I usually take his questions seriously, trying my best to answer them, even if I must resort to Googling or guessing. I was driving and couldn't use the first technique, so I considered the second. But there's nothing inherently malevolent in a number, is there?

"I ... uh, don't know," I finally admitted. He was, unsurprisingly, unsatisfied, and wanted examples of when 13 would be unlucky.

"Well, you're not supposed to have 13 people at a dinner party," I said, realizing as soon as the words were out of my mouth that he would have no idea what that means. Even before COVID, I would never have willingly let anyone old enough to vote see my home's condition.

"Or a hotel," I added, quickly, before he could start in with the questions about why his parents don't have dinner parties or adult friends or meals that don't include mac and cheese. "There's usually no 13th floor in a hotel."

He was blown away.

"How do they not make a 13th floor?" he marveled,

picturing a building with a gaping hole where the offending story would have been.

"Well, they make one," I said. "They just call it the 14th floor."

"But that's tricking people!" he exclaimed, offended.

"Everyone knows it's really the 13th floor."

And though he found that strange, I explained that it's that way with all superstitions: The superstitious are all kind of tricking themselves — and I know from firsthand experience.

Because I exist in that same weird in-between land, the place where I do superstitious things like cross myself before icons and knock on wood, while also not believing any of it helps.

"What could it hurt?" I think as I chase my kids around the dining room with handfuls of salt to throw over their shoulders.

(They hate it, the salt thing, and the more they run away, the more I insist. I'd feel terrible, after all, if one of them fell off the slide and broke his arm because I failed that day to properly season him.)

Before the kids were born, I underwent IVF looking like Mr. T, so covered in chains I could barely lift my head. For each appointment, I wore my baptismal cross, my grandmother's wedding ring, a replica Alexander the Great coin and a gold cartouche engraved with a Libra scales symbol.

And I don't even believe in astrology!

Well, for a while, in high school, I was really into astrology. I read my horoscope and asked potential crushes what their sign was, until it occurred to me the whole thing was easily debunked by the existence of time twins.

But by the time I was old enough to have trouble having kids, I didn't believe it anymore.

That hasn't stopped me, though, and it never will.

Maybe it's my Greekness.

In Greece, old ladies spit at cute babies, but it's only to keep the bad luck away.

"What a sweetie!" they say, quickly hocking a loogie so no evil spirits accidentally put the evil eye on him. "Ptu! Ptu!"

It's just the polite thing to do. And what could it hurt?

I admit, it makes no sense, but, in the grand scheme of things, we control so little in this world. We can't control how smart or happy or rich we'll be. We can't control births or deaths or who falls in love with us or doesn't.

We sure as heck can control, however, whether we open an umbrella in the house.

And that's why, when my kids are grown, the baby clothes are all donated and the house no longer looks like a toy warehouse, I'm sure I'll start having dinner parties.

But when I'm making the guest list, there will never, ever be 13 names on it.

It's superstitious, yes, but it's also one risk factor I can mitigate.

And, really, what could a little superstition hurt?

Pandemania

Daily Work Log for Garvey, Inc., Quarantine Edition

April 16, 2020

Dear shareholders,

In this troubled time, we at Garvey, Inc., offer a small window into company operations as we move all activity off-site. The following log details a typical workday as Garvey, Inc., as employees and executives manage this unprecedented crisis.

7:15 a.m. One of the company's low-level employees, newly promoted to "Junior Short Person," enters the sleep cubicle shared by the CEM (Chief Executive Mother) and CEF (Chief Executive Father). Junior Short Person (JSP), a real self-starter, displays eagerness to begin work. JSP uses best practices to evict CEM and CEF from bed. JSP pulls CEM's eyelids apart, yelling "WAKE UP" until all attempt at further sleep ends due to low return on investment.

7:30 a.m. The second employee of Garvey, Inc., "Assistant Junior Short Person" (AJSP), awakens. AJSP lacks the seniority to be trained on the toilet machinery so for now management changes his diapers, something that - though arguably below pay grade for C-level executives - was both included in the job description and addressed in the interview process.

7:45 a.m. One of the Garvey, Inc., employees, JSP, expresses dissatisfaction with his supervisors' lack of support for his choices in office attire. JSP throws himself to the ground to protest the decision not to allow him to wear pajamas all day, every day, for the duration of his employment. The company negotiates with JSP to allow one (1) pajama day a week. The communications department sends out a congratulatory email about the win.

8 a.m. A minor kerfuffle breaks out over the executive suite's decision not to allow leftover Easter candy to be consumed at breakfast.

9 a.m. The new employee training program called "distance learning" continues to flummox upper management. Organizations such as schools, libraries, museums and park districts flood supervisors with "helpful" emails. Suggestions for activities include reproducing John Singer Sargent sketches with homemade charcoal, teaching Japanese to preschoolers in three easy hours a day and building a scale treehouse version of Frank Lloyd Wright's "Fallingwater." Supervisors, gripped with guilt, delete the emails unread and instead put on a YouTube video of kids' yoga exercises.

10 a.m. The CEM is sent to HR to discuss her repeated references to employees being "short."

Noon Lunch break. Negotiations restart with the employees over when Easter candy may be eaten. Executives acknowledge that the temptation of staring at the Easter baskets while eating lunch may be too much for some employees to handle. All agree to restructure the dinner table layout until further notice so there are no chocolate bunnies in the work area.

1 p.m. The executives use both employees' nap time to complete freelance assignments for outside companies, also known as "doing their jobs."

3 p.m. One of the executives accidentally replies-all to an email for her "job," and as her "boss" calls to discuss the email on speakerphone, JSP enters the room to inform the CEM, quite loudly, that he needs his "butt wiped" because he "pooped."

4 p.m. More distance learning, via singalong of "Head, Shoulders, Knees and Toes," followed by art time, during which significant portions of company property are threatened with destruction via markers deceptively labeled "washable." Management imposition of clean-up time gets poor approval ratings from both employees. Executives threaten to bring up the lack of cooperation in upcoming performance reviews.

5 p.m. The arrival of "TV time" is greeted with enthusiasm by both employees of Garvey, Inc. Executives briefly adjourn to Twitter, then prepare for the sunset rush hour. During menu development, CEM and CEF agree to the inclusion of vegetables despite past surveys showing low consumption rates.

6 p.m. Dinner, consisting mostly of jellybeans parceled out between negotiated bites of chicken nuggets, is eaten.

7 p.m. Bath time presents more opportunities for conflict resolution after both Garvey, Inc., employees demand the same yellow boat. Additionally, AJSP won't stop drinking the dirty bathwater, leading to an early adjournment.

8 p.m. Negotiations resume on the number and quality of songs and stories included in the employees' bedtime routine. The employees achieve two (2) more readings of "The Very Hungry Caterpillar," after which a total of five (5) questions are allowed on the pupation, feeding and growth of caterpillars and one (1) follow-up question about whether the company will allow employees to have a pet butterfly. The answer is determined to be no as "butterflies are outside creatures." Complaints are logged.

9 p.m. JSP continues to display insubordinate behavior, getting out of bed and sneaking downstairs repeatedly under pretenses of being "thirsty" or needing to "go potty." He is directed to the employee handbook, where bedtimes are clearly stated. Exhaustion reigns throughout the company and both executives fall asleep while auditing "The Mandalorian," leading to an early cessation of all activity.

10 p.m. Another successful workday at Garvey, Inc., is concluded.

Garvey, Inc., employees and executives hope all shareholders stay safe and healthy, and that regular operations resume forthwith.

(c) 2023 Pioneer Press. All rights reserved. Distributed by Tribune Content Agency, LLC

Why Are We in Quarantine? We're Saving the Lives of People We Will Never Meet.

April 24, 2020

Every day, an email hits my inbox from the Cook County medical examiner's office. In it are the names and cause of deaths of every county resident whose death led to an investigation.

Lately, those emails have gotten longer. Where they were once two or three pages, they've increased to 16, 17, 18 pages, full of names. Almost all have the same cause of death, COVID-19. The vast majority are older people, many with complicating factors like diabetes, heart disease, renal failure, cancer.

It can be tempting to see the deaths as sad but inevitable, merely a hastening of a demise that loomed, imminently, even before the crisis. But in those lists, I see my grandmother.

Katerina Evdoxiadis was born and lived in Oktonia, a mountainous village off the eastern coast of mainland Greece.

To phenomenally understate it, she worked hard, as a subsistence farmer and as the mother to four boys. In a place and a time where a man did not help his wife with housework, cooking or childcare, she shouldered the burden for six people. As a baby, my father, hung in swaddling clothes from a nearby tree, watched as she worked in the fields.

She mourned never having a daughter, and when my family moved in with her and my grandfather in the 1980s, my grandmother lavished affection on me.

She was a hard woman, generally, having earned the nickname "The Hairdresser" in her youth after she dragged into the street a woman having an affair with my grandfather and chopped off her locks in full view of the assembled villagers.

But she was my most ardent protector, my vengeful Greek goddess of a "Yia-Yia."

I remember sitting at her kitchen table as she fed me glykes, my little brother banging on the locked door to be let in, while she called me "manaraki mou," "my littlest lamb," and petted my hair.

On the day we left and moved back to the U.S., my grandmother wept fiercely. She didn't know if we'd ever be back, but return we did, fairly regularly, throughout my childhood.

Later, when I was in my 20s, she had the first of a series of strokes. I didn't have enough money for a ticket to visit, didn't know how serious her condition was, and by the time I made it, she was fundamentally changed.

Mostly paralyzed, she was unable to talk, walk or feed herself. My father warned me when I went into the room what to expect, but it still hit me full-force.

My grandmother, once muscular and thick from work in the fields, was as slight as a bird. The skin was stretched across her face, as thin as parchment.

She turned her head to look at me and I could get out no more than a choked, "Yia-Yia" before I began to sob. I cried because she looked so sick, because I hadn't come earlier, because I was afraid of her and because I was embarrassed at my reaction.

When I could speak again, I took her hand, apologized and whispered to her that I loved her, over and over again. I was too upset, and my Greek had degraded too much, to say anything else. My grandmother never turned her eyes from me, just stared, unblinking, until her caregiver had to physically move her head so she would eat.

I told my father that I felt my grandmother had known I was there, had seen and recognized me.

"No," he said sadly, shaking his head. "The doctor says she doesn't understand anything anymore."

Maybe that's true. Or maybe a couple of synapses fired when she saw me, and a hazy image floated through her mind, one of me on her lap, eating sweets, all those years ago, in her kitchen. Maybe she had been waiting for me, to see me one last time.

A couple of months later, she died, and I returned to the village for her funeral.

When I kissed her unlined forehead as she lay in the casket, it was cold and hard. There was nothing left of the woman I loved but I felt gratitude that I'd seen her, gratitude that she'd gotten to see me.

She had been on the razor's edge of death for some time, so perhaps it's ignorant or silly to think that she held out to hear my voice again before she died. But I do.

So, to my point: Those of you who are staying at home these days, those who are social distancing, who are wearing masks and washing your hands, you're saving lives. But you won't ever meet the people you've saved.

I therefore invite you to pretend as if you're saving Katerina Evdoxiadis, as if you're giving her, though she may be broken and old and dying, the chance to live for just a bit longer.

You may never have caught COVID-19, or it might have been no more than a bad cold for you. But by staying home and taking precautions when you do go out, you're giving a gift to many people like my grandmother, giving them the gift of a chance at living longer than they might otherwise.

You are also giving another, perhaps more powerful gift to someone who loves those people: Time.

Time for a granddaughter to save up for a plane ticket to visit, time for a sister to forgive old arguments, time for a son to mature enough to know that, despite his father's flaws, he tried.

You're giving a cousin, or a brother, or a friend a chance to be in the room when they die. You're giving the possibility of a funeral where friends and family can mourn, can hug and comfort each other.

We are all fatally ill, are all born to die. What could mean more to us than another decade, another year, another day, another chance to do the right thing, to apologize, to kiss, to hug, to say "I love you"?

For many of us, whatever patience we had with isolation and boredom is in tatters. We've blown through our Netflix queue and run out of activities for the kids. Even the walks outside are repetitive. The impact of the changes we've made can be hard to visualize.

But I remember that day in Oktonia, when I saw my grandmother alive for the last time, and I know the value of the sacrifice we're making.

After all, we might never do anything more beautiful, more selfless or more meaningful in our entire lives.

(c) 2023 Pioneer Press. All rights reserved. Distributed by Tribune Content Agency, LLC.

How Am I? Let's Start With the Ghost Faucet and Go From There

August 17, 2020

I'm considering taking "how are you?" out of rotation as a greeting.

Not because I don't care - I do! I really do! - but because I've realized that being on the other end of that question leaves you in a tough spot.

You can either answer, "I'm fine," a brazen lie, or you can tell the truth:

There are spiderwebs on the inside of my car, I'm fighting with my kitchen sink's faucet, one of our kids has been emotionally scarred from finding out how black holes are made, the other is making excellent progress on a journey toward an all-fruit-snack-and-milk diet and I recently realized that my Kindle isn't actually super blurry because it's broken but maybe, instead, perhaps I see just a (tiny) bit better with the help of some - ahem - reading glasses.

We've also recently come to terms with our choice as a family for at least one semester of remote learning, a time that promises to be remote in many ways including how far removed it will be from actual learning.

I can't work myself up to get too mad at the the teachers. I mean, I don't envy anyone trying to get preschoolers to responsibly use the "mute" function on Zoom. And I think my kid, who can capably discuss the reasons behind the International Astronomical Union's 2006 decision to downgrade Pluto to dwarf planet status, will probably be OK. I know plenty of other children won't be, though.

I still don't understand why the choices are either "create a Petri dish to explore how best to transmit coronavirus" or "plop your kid in front of a computer for hours at a time for the thrill ride that is 'watching an adult talk.'" Even if we threw 95% of the world's scientists at developing a vaccine, surely we could spare one or two to figure out how to make videoconferencing school less boring.

Another frequent intruder on my daily peace of mind is the misbehavior of our tempestuous faucet, the "Ladylux." Yes, that's really her name and the more I think about it, the more fitting it is. She's pretty, sort of, in an overdone kind of way, and she was shockingly expensive. Like a Real Housewife of Wherever, she's too fancy for her surroundings and seems to relish causing drama. She has a "touch" feature that's supposed to be high-tech and impressive but is mostly infuriating.

At first, she'd turn on and off randomly, something I learned were called "ghost" turn-ons. When I complained about that, and about how sometimes the water wouldn't stop running even if the handle was in the "off" position, my husband pushed back.

"You just need to learn how to use it," he said, suggesting I sit down with the instruction manual sometime. My protests that I would prefer a faucet that doesn't require training went unanswered.

I'm also a bit - oh, what's the word? - furious that we have a faucet that will eventually need a battery change. We're the parents of two kids under 5. We have to change batteries in trains, trucks and dinosaurs that spit plastic balls out of their mouths, I wish we didn't have to do the same with our sink.

I also should mention that the faucet is beloved by my husband in a way that doesn't seem totally appropriate.

I tried to get a video of the faucet turning on and off but the second I whipped out my phone, she started behaving. Not a single ghost sputter or spit in sight.

Eventually, my husband kind of fixed the faucet, but she still doesn't reliably function correctly. Apparently there's something in our sink that's coated with something bad? I'm not educated enough to understand it.

"I hate the faucet," I confessed to my husband, who then looked at me strangely.

"I hate it, too," he finally admitted.

It looks like we're going to be stuck in the house for a while. My company announced recently that we'd probably be working from home until well into 2021. It's gotten to the point where I don't even miss leaving the house anymore. So I guess we'll just be here, watching our two monkey children climbing all over the house, manically slapping our faucet to get it to shut off, for another six months.

On the plus side, though, my dad did win a goat in his village lottery.

I was a little worried about what he'd do with it when he came back to the U.S. from Greece after summer was over.

"What are you going to do with the goat?" I asked, thinking he'd pawn it off on some villager to watch for the winter.

He laughed.

"What do you think? I'm going to cook it and eat it!"

Problem solved, I suppose.

Anyway, this all seems like a lot to lay on someone when they call to chitchat and ask after the kids. It's kind of a long-winded response to "How are you?"

Maybe from here on out, I'll just stick with the classics:

"I'm fine! How are you?"

(c) 2023 Pioneer Press. All rights reserved. Distributed by Tribune Content Agency, LLC.

When It Comes to Vaccines, It's a Matter of Trust

October 30, 2021

After the first day of kindergarten, my son asked me each day, for weeks, why he had to go to school.

"Because you need to learn," I told him.

"I can learn at home," he replied.

"Because we want you to make friends," we tried.

"I already have friends," he responded.

"Because Mom and Dad will get in trouble if you don't go to school," we explained.

"You can teach me at home." Volley returned.

Finally, desperately, I resorted to words that I'd heard so often from my own parents I vowed never to repeat them:

"Because I said so."

It's come to that. I anticipate I'll soon be complaining about the prices at restaurants and needing help with the remote control.

But even if that's true, even if I am slowly turning into my mother, I'm seeing the wisdom of "Because I said so" more lately — particularly, for example, when I think about mask and vaccine mandates.

For those who refuse, it's not enough to hear from epidemiologists and public health professionals that masking and vaccines, particularly when some are too young to be vaccinated and many health conditions lower vaccine efficacy, are crucial to stopping COVID.

It's not enough because, thanks to our solipsistic culture, we've convinced ourselves that we must be convinced to follow the rules.

We must comprehend. We must agree.

Admittedly, blind obedience to authority has its dangers, and the government is not our Mommy and Daddy. I understand, if not share, the impulse to view with skepticism new and complex science. I appreciate, if not share, the thinking that, with enough research, we can educate ourselves in all matters.

But we all put our faith in others, in experts, in those who have training or education or experience that we lack. We all trust.

We trust the carpenters who build our homes, trust that they know more about erecting sturdy structures than we do.

We trust the engineers who design our cars, trust that they've tested the seat belts and airbags to protect us in a crash.

We trust the cooks in restaurants, trust that they've handled the food safely and sanitized their equipment to avoid getting us sick.

We trust because we must. Because we can't do it all, can't know it all, can't be it all.

There are missing pieces in all of us. It's why we marry. It's why we adopt dogs and have children, why we attend church and read books and listen to music.

We need love. We need to be entertained and inspired and distracted. We need the pieces we lack, and we get them from outside ourselves.

Without these missing pieces — and the pieces are different for each of us — we cannot live our lives as they're meant to be lived. To complete ourselves, our lives, we need other people and other things.

If that's too esoteric for you, how about this?

Society is a division of labor, like the one in my house

where my husband washes the dishes and I do the laundry. The compartmentalization lubricates the machinery of daily life. It also strengthens our bonds to need each other, to rely on someone else.

The labor done by doctors, scientists and drug manufacturers over the last 18 months has been nothing short of miraculous. They have developed lifesaving treatments and preventative medicine, and in the gigantic family that is our society, we now must do our part. We do it to protect ourselves, but more importantly, to protect us all.

Ultimately, when we ask ourselves "Why?" the answer is simple: Because they said so.

It's the Season of Giving — Isn't It?

December 4, 2021

I'm not normally a holiday crank, but year two of A Very COVID Christmas has me feeling slightly Ebenezer Scrooge-ish.

Last year, we missed a great deal, but there was a warmth, a kindness in the air from a wartime unity. Holiday routines were altered but offered respite from the sadness and isolation.

But in winter 2021, the grim pandemic realities have gone nowhere. While people are traveling and big dinners are scheduled again, the cruelties of our increasingly fractured society remain. All Christmas, no charity.

Take the "supply chain" controversy inspiring rage across the country. If you listened to politicians and pundits, you'd think our grocery store shelves were bare, that we wait months for necessities.

The reality, however, is that our selection of ready merchandise has been slightly and temporarily reduced. Have we become so spoiled that even a worldwide pandemic is no excuse for the smallest disruption to our consumption? Can we withstand no frustration, regardless how mild?

We talk about inflation, as if 5 million people hadn't died, three quarters of a million in our country alone. We don't mention the millions of American women who had to leave jobs to care for their children. We ignore the untold numbers of workers who quit after two years of being jerked around, furloughed one minute and working overtime the next: the airline stewards and massage therapists and fast-food employees screamed at for enforcing mask rules, the waiters (federal minimum wage: $2.13 an hour) whose employment became unpredictable as their frustrations skyrocketed.

Isn't it healthy to rethink life in the face of death, to quit your job, to go back to school, to spend more time with family? Is it wrong that people are increasingly less interested in working unfulfilling, demanding jobs that pay poorly and offer few benefits?

It doesn't feel very Christmas-y to prioritize the stock market's unceasing growth over human lives. But maybe that's the "bah humbug" in me. Maybe I just don't get the joy of unfettered capitalism.

Otherwise, I'd understand how people furious at pandemic restrictions could refuse to take a simple, free action to help end them.

It's like we're all standing outside of our burning house. There's a lake nearby, brimming with water. A third of us, though, won't even pick up a bucket.

"You can't make me," they say.

Yes, but can we beg? Can we plead? Can we, weary of all these variants and delays and deaths, ask you to help yourself, if no one else?

Do we have to keep watching our stuff burning up inside?

Humankind shared a collective, horrible experience these last couple of years, but it has not united us. We see before us the evidence of our human frailty, the proof that our squabbles are temporal and transitory, but, somehow, we're more self-obsessed than ever.

The enmity is enough to make me long for The War Against the War On Christmas, when people wished you "Merry Christmas" (heavy emphasis on the word "Christmas") with such vehemence it sounded less a seasonal greeting and more a threat of bodily harm.

Yes, there's warmth inside the walls of my home, from our fireplace and from the hugs of my family, from the baking fruitcake and the mulling cider. That I can control; that I can make so.

But my Christmas wish is that we could find a way to extend the walls of our homes outward, in our minds, further and further, until they reach the limits of our towns, our states, our countries, until they reach the end of the world.

Then, maybe, we would see every living being as a member of our household, our family. We would love them as we love our families, as we love ourselves.

And *that* would be a merry Christmas indeed.

'Socialized Medicine' Can't Be Any Worse Than This

January 22, 2022

About 30 years ago, when the Clinton Administration began looking at how to reform our floundering health care system, the idea emerged for a "single payer" — in this case, the federal government — to provide health insurance for all.

Plenty of wealthy, capitalist nations comparable to the United States — the United Kingdom, Canada — have single-payer models, to overwhelming success. Everyone gets treatment, no one loses their house or car to pay for medical bills and a certain level of health care is guaranteed.

The downside, we were told (by those who wished to torpedo the plan), was that we would get — and here you'll have to imagine a scary, booming voice saying the words — *socialized medicine*.

Socialized medicine, unlike the socialized fire departments, socialized police forces and socialized school systems we already have and enjoy, was bad, bad, bad.

We would get "rationed care." We'd wait for tests and treatment. Quality would suffer. We'd drown in bureaucracy and paperwork. Doctors would hate it. There would even be committees set up to determine whether someone would get life-saving care — so-called death panels.

Decades after these tactics first were used to gin up electoral anxiety, the worst outcomes they threatened have come true — not in any kind of "socialized" health care system, but one nourished under the wing of unrestricted capitalism.

You've probably seen this in your own life: You've waited interminable lengths of time to see a specialist, like one person I know who couldn't get in to see a cardiologist for three months or another who had to wait months for a GI appointment and then another two months for a colonoscopy.

You've had to fill out interminable forms, acknowledgments and releases, such as the three-page-long one Cigna required for COVID-test reimbursement, recently tweeted out by writer and activist Cory Doctorow.

You've battled with hospitals or your insurance company (or, lucky you, both!) to get some necessary treatment covered or paid for. My husband and I are still trying to iron out some mysterious problem preventing our insurance from paying a $1,000 bill for tests my son had more than a year ago.

You've seen or heard of doctors, infuriated by the way insurance companies manage every aspect of patients' treatment, quitting the profession entirely or giving up on being able to provide the kind of care they know is possible, like one particularly fed-up doctor who tore into United Healthcare when they denied coverage of a nausea medication for a child undergoing chemotherapy.

As for death panels, health insurance companies are already talking about pulling back coverage of emergency room visits they don't deem necessary, causing people to second-guess going to the ER for ailments that could kill them without prompt treatment. If you knew when you were having a heart attack, after all, you'd work in the ER yourself.

My point, therefore, is simple: If we're going to have the bad parts of socialism, why can't we at least get the medicine to go with it?

There'll be nothing to prevent people from getting private insurance if they want it and can afford it. If someone enjoys being put on hold for an hour to talk to a "customer service" representative about why they need their blood pressure medication, they'll be free to keep doing that!

The rest of us, though, can have some stability, some consistency and some reassurance that when we need to see a doctor, when we need a medication, when we think we should go to the ER, that we can.

We will know it will be paid for.

We will know that we won't go bankrupt because we or a family member had the bad luck to get sick.

If we want the terrible, horrible, no-good, very bad socialized medicine, we should have it. After all, it can't get any worse than it is now.

A Simple Proposal From a Resident of London in 1941: Let's Give Up On World War II

February 5, 2022

Feb. 3, 1941
To the editor of The Daily Mirror,
It is with a profound sense of dismay that I write today to announce that I, a resident of 1940s London, tire of World War II.

It's been practically years of this nonsense, fighting and drafts and nonstop pitching in together as a nation, and in my opinion — and that of a great many other fine citizens of the British Empire — it's high time we all get back to normal.

I'm sick of the rationing — butter and meat and sugar — and the government telling me how much I can buy of seemingly every item on my shopping list and what I'll pay for the privilege of doing so. If I have the money (and I do!), shouldn't I be able to eat as many banana splits as I want, availability of crucial goods for Allied troops be damned?

Everyone's talking about fascism lately, but I say the real fascists are those trying to stop me from buying more than a pound of bacon a week.

And what's all this about shipping routes and trade embargoes and supply chain disruption? We're supposed to only eat cakes and other sweet treats at special occasions just because there's a war on? Winston Churchill may be a decent public speaker but he's obviously a terrible national leader if he can't ensure a wide enough variety of food available for my breakfast buffet.

I also find the continued nighttime blackouts to be profoundly annoying.

For months, I've been fine with turning off our family's lights at dusk to prevent the Luftwaffe from being able to discern the military targets in the city, but, frankly, it's getting old.

My children can't do their homework in darkness. And when you weigh the negative effects on their studies against the very small chance of fiery death from above, I'm starting to think it's not worth the trade-off.

I'm an adult. If I want to take the risk of turning on my lights during the blitzkrieg, I should have the freedom to do so.

Enough finger-wagging from soldiers on the front lines about whether I'm doing my part at home. No one forced them to join up. Well, perhaps they did, but one can always depart without leave and stand trial for desertion, can't one?

Additionally, I don't appreciate being shamed for having political opinions that go against the grain.

I'm an independent and I do my own research. I don't just accept the word of any old media hack who tries to tell me that German paramilitary forces are carrying out pogroms against Jewish people. I guess I just need a little more evidence than the sheeple who believe everything they're told.

Yes, I admit it, I listen to Axis-sympathizing radio broadcasters and, yes, one did call Adolf Hitler "a scamp who, despite being a bit naughty lately, almost certainly has no plans to annex Yugoslavia." But these broadcasters have a right to free speech and should be able to say whatever they like, even if their assertions are dangerous to my safety, detrimental to the war effort or even, let's say, *slightly* treasonous.

What are we fighting this war for, if not for the right of someone to make godawful amounts of money telling me things that upset and frighten me, things that are both demonstrably untrue and politically divisive?

In conclusion, I propose that we end all this claptrap and simply snap our fingers and go back to the way I vaguely remember things were like before the war began. Our brilliant British scientists should be spending less time trying to break German codes and more time developing a time machine that can transport us back to 1938.

Keep Britain great.
Yours very truly,
Nigel Farraday

Ending Vaccine and Mask Mandates Should Be Done Slowly — and With Empathy

February 19, 2022

If you want to understand parents terrified about schools ending mask mandates, maybe it will help to explain why I hate nuts.

A few years ago, I edited a newspaper story about a child who choked and died at a pool.

The boy was about the same age as my son at the time, and the imagery — of a happy, playing kid asking his mom for a snack and then, a minute later, choking to death on a nut — has lived in my mind ever since.

For years after editing that story, I wouldn't let my kids touch nuts. Now that they're older, they can have peanuts or cashews — if they're in smaller pieces, and I watch them while they eat.

My older son also almost choked once, on pancakes of all things, and the cold terror I felt in that moment has remained with me.

Now, the more time that's passed, the more I've loosened up. But I still worry about choking, and every time they cough while they're eating, the fear rushes back.

I don't know what the statistics are on children choking to death, and, frankly, it wouldn't much matter. It wouldn't reassure me in the slightest to know that my kid's death was a statistical anomaly. And I realize that I'm transmitting my anxiety to my children. They see other kids eating grapes and hot dogs without their mom first hacking at the food as if it was attacking them. They must know that I worry.

But it's been all too easy for me to picture being the mother of that boy, forever frozen in time, wracked with guilt and misery, and I can see his death in my mind. The emotion is insistent, will not be denied.

For some, that's also the way it goes with COVID.

Some people feel, strongly and presently, the danger of COVID — to themselves, to their kids, to their relatives and friends.

The data, how likely they are to catch it, how likely they are to be hospitalized and die, is less important than the emotion, the urgency of fear.

Arguing the statistics, being rude or dismissive, isn't the way to win over these people. We must instead lead with empathy. We need to understand that planning and preparation are key in ending mask and vaccine mandates. And, for some people, we must wait.

We should talk about taking off masks and going back to "normal" gently, recognizing the emotion present in the conversation.

We can, yes, talk more about the risks, small and large, that we all accept to fully live our lives. We can point out that we can't get very far — both figuratively and literally — if we refuse to drive a car, swim in the ocean or let our kids eat a nut.

But we also need to understand that everyone has different tolerances for risk. Some of us will climb Mount Everest, knowing that we might never come down. Others won't fly on planes for fear of crashing.

Similarly, one parent might tell their child to mask up at school and another won't. They have different risk tolerance, different beliefs about whether taking those risks is necessary.

We're past the point where COVID's risk is inarguable. We

have vaccines and therapeutics. We know more about the disease than we did two years ago.

In February of 2022, COVID's danger varies.

Some of us are immunocompromised. Some of us have high-risk relatives. Some of us simply could not live with ourselves if our loved ones or community members were the statistical outliers who wound up hospitalized or dead.

We all, eventually, will have to decide for ourselves, and we will have to let others decide for themselves, too.

We'll either let our kids eat the nut or we won't, but hopefully, we will view with empathy different choices. Because we all want the best for those we love.

Easy Answers Elude Us as Mask and Vaccine Mandates Fall

April 23, 2022

COVID isn't over, and it never will be.

Even if the disease goes the way of smallpox (which isn't as gone as it used to be), there will still be bloody arguments about masking, vaccines and whether it's OK to make anyone take even the tiniest protective measure for another human being's welfare. These conflicts haven't been resolved, and never will be.

Though clear answers elude us, mask and vaccine mandates seem destined to the past, despite the federal government challenging the ruling ending airline mask rules.

Those mandates are long gone, and it's not because they were unfair or overly intrusive. They're done because, as a nation, we have been through it.

"It" being "the wringer."

"It" being more than two years of death, lockdowns and shutdowns, business failures and marriage failures. We've been drinking and eating too much. We've been looking at too many screens and wearing too many elastic-waist clothes.

Our kids are turning feral.

I took mine to the library recently and saw it firsthand. They ran and screamed, lay down and pushed every button in sight until I almost literally dragged them out.

"What is wrong with you kids?" I thought as they bounced off the walls.

Then I remembered: *Oh. They haven't been in a library for two years.*

And the kids aren't the only ones losing it.

Driving manners are unbelievably foul lately. There's a crosswalk near my home, and no matter how many kids in bikes wait patiently to cross, cars still fly through at 40 miles per hour.

I had someone almost hunt me down, rabid with road rage, after I didn't see him and cut him off.

"I'm sorry!" I mouthed, waving to say that I hadn't meant to turn in front of him.

Still, he lay on his horn, tailgating me for blocks, revving his engine behind me at a stoplight until it turned green and he could scream something unintelligible while swerving into the turn lane to pass.

Now, this is not to say that these minor things — amped kids and mean drivers — are entirely new, and they're certainly not worth anyone's life. But the landscape has changed, dramatically, regarding COVID in the last two years.

There are vaccines and therapeutics. The dominant strain appears to be more contagious but less deadly. Cases might tick up, but deaths are comparatively low, and we will never — could never — get either number to zero.

We know vastly more about the disease (though we still don't know everything) and it's become clear that zero-COVID goals are fantasies.

Most importantly, though, we won't be able to put the genie back in the bottle without overwhelming need and even more overwhelming evidence that these measures work.

That's impossible in 2022, when even the most learned scientists are subject to questioning from those educated at Facebook University.

Even if we *could* somehow manage to persuade the more liberal half of the country, a good portion of the other half reflexively rejects any measure or belief solely because it's espoused by

Democrats. It's a game of one-upmanship that no one ever wins.

Maybe this sounds depressing. But easy answers are for children.

My son likes to ask me, "Is he a good guy or a bad guy?"

In cartoons, it's easy to figure out.

If he's got slanted eyebrows and skinny arms, he's a bad guy. In real life, though, figuring out right and wrong, good and evil, is tougher.

Once you become an adult, the clarity of childhood fades quickly.

So, we muddle through, as best we can, together.

And we hope that the choices we've made, which are sometimes not choices at all, turn out to be for the best.

Because, either way, it's the next generation who will face the consequences.

During COVID-19, Parents Have Been Hung Out To Dry

May 28, 2022

Either parenting has gotten exponentially harder in the last two-plus years, or I've developed in that same time Olympic-level complaining skills.

I'm willing to accept the latter possibility if everyone else accepts the former.

I'm also willing to accept that it's gotten harder to be anything in this country: a neighbor, a co-worker, a person who keeps their cool in the checkout line at the grocery store.

Parents don't have a monopoly on stress.

But lately, it seems as if those in power, elected officials who can actually do something about formula shortages and school shootings and COVID-19 shutdowns, remain willfully ignorant about the way parents have been repeatedly hit by a bus for two years straight.

In the beginning of COVID-19's quarantine era, there was a lot of talk about heroic teachers and doctors — and, God love them, they did and do magnificent work — but little understanding of the way parents had picked up entire second professions (imagine what it was like to be a doctor or a teacher *and* a parent).

In addition to what was already untenable — the ever-increasing demands to provide the perfect financial, emotional, spiritual, nutritional and material upbringing — parents had to home-school, as well.

Then, perhaps not so mysteriously, many became enraged over continued school shutdowns. Parents screamed at school board meetings, marched on suburban streets and fumed on Facebook.

And though their rage was misplaced and weaponized by callous conservative activists, it was also profoundly understandable.

Because during the pandemic, working parents — working *anybodies,* actually — have gotten almost no real help.

There were no emergency parental leave measures, no help with the developing child-care crisis — no solutions for day cares without qualified workers, no solutions to the suddenly skyrocketing wages for babysitters and nannies. There were no guaranteed emergency child-care days and no right to work remotely.

Stimulus and unemployment checks were insignificant in every way. Many couldn't return to inflexible work environments, and those who did made impossible, daily choices about whether to prioritize their sanity, their finances or their children.

We got through however we could, long-term consequences be damned.

Everyone — not just, but especially, parents — mistreated their bodies and lived under pressure, and now, as society is reopening, there's no help transitioning.

Did you let your health go to pot because you were afraid of going to the doctor or because it was impossible to get an appointment? Would health care clinics, free checkups or streamlined insurance claim procedures help?

Too bad. Hope you enjoy the same exorbitant health care bills and bureaucratic insurance hassles as before the pandemic!

Did you gain weight or rely too much on gambling, alcohol or drugs? Would subsidized gym memberships, meditation classes or rehabilitation programs be nice?

Well, sure they would, but so would free unicorn rides, and you're not getting those either!

Were you lonely, isolated? Are you longing to visit family and friends but can't afford the rising costs of flights, gasoline or hotels? Maybe coupons or discounts sound good.

That's unfortunate, because as a citizen of the United States of America, it's your responsibility to understand that the health and happiness of large corporations is far more important than your own.

And now, NOW, parents are grappling with the very real danger that their children may be assassinated at school by a teenager able to legally purchase military-grade weaponry.

"We have to act," the president said, and as little as it was, it was more than many other craven politicians, frantically running away from news cameras.

Meanwhile, parents wait. Wait for help, wait for hope. Wait for words to magically transform into deeds.

It's increasingly clear that if parents want anything done, just like with the laundry, our only choice is to do it ourselves.

And, as is often true with the laundry at my house, I just don't know if I have the energy.

The Pandemic Is Over but the Sickness Has Just Begun

September 24, 2022

The pandemic is over.

How do I know?

Not because COVID has gone away — no, I realize that many are still getting sick and even dying from the virus — and not because we no longer mask up or get booster shots (in fact, I just wore a mask at the doctor's office today and am scheduling family boosters for next month).

No, I know the pandemic is over because fall has, once again, become an unbroken string of sicknesses working its way through the inhabitants of our house for months on end.

These minor but annoying illnesses disappeared for years. After all, we were mostly isolated, only venturing out when everyone was masked, vaccinated, outside or (during the worst of the pandemic) all three. During those halcyon days, the kids didn't have so much as a sniffle, let alone the parade of weirdo childhood illnesses like roseola and fifth disease.

Now we're back to explaining to the grandparents that, no, hand, foot and mouth disease isn't something farm animals get but is instead one of those childhood illnesses that they and everyone else probably had by the time they were 2.

For the last couple of years, kids have mostly been sheltered from other kids, who carry germs home the same way they transport leaves and rocks from the park.

But I'm remembering now what it was like in the Before Days, when our oldest went to day care for the first time. I'm remembering how he was sick, almost nonstop, from November to April, one time even simultaneously getting strep throat and hand, foot and mouth, and I'm dreading something similar this year.

We've already been through a metric ton of COVID tests (all negative), popsicles and children's Tylenol. We've been to urgent care and the pediatrician's office and (during one particularly rough night) the ER at the children's hospital.

We get messages from school and where they used to only warn of COVID outbreaks, now they talk of strep and RSV and flu — even lice (shudder). In the spring of 2020, the chances that your kids would get close enough to a non-family member to catch something like lice were nil to none.

But the pandemic is over. Those days are gone.

I realized when we sent the kids to school this year that we'd be in for it.

"They're going to get sick," I warned my husband. Their immune systems, particularly our younger son's, whose early childhood has been spent sheltered by the umbrella of COVID restrictions, just hadn't gotten the workout they needed. But they'd have to be exposed to the world sooner or later.

It'll be like ripping off a bandage, I told myself. A couple of months of runny noses and a few days out from school and then they'd be fine.

Instead, they've spent so much time at home that they now thrill to hear that they're running a temperature, knowing it means a day away from school, one full of TV and eating whatever they want.

I told the younger one that he'd be going back to school after his second timeout in three weeks.

"I'm going to be sick tomorrow," he said with a smile.

He coughed artfully at breakfast and made sure I took

note.

"I'm coughing!" he hollered while I was in the kitchen packing up their lunches.

"You're still going to school!" I hollered back.

For like a march through the muck, there's no stopping now.

We must continue, no matter how long our trip through The Land of Kid Disease takes, no matter how bedraggled we are when we get there.

After all, we should be happy. The pandemic is over.

What a relief, right?

No One Is Owed an Apology for Mask Mandates

February 25, 2023

It's fashionable these days among conservatives to look back on the early days of COVID with smug self-congratulations.

"See? We, those who said that masks were 'face diapers' and who screamed at grocery store workers over mask rules were correct. Those mask mandates did nothing. It was you, the government and liberals, who were wrong to shame us for noncompliance."

Witness the recent New York Times column by Bret Stephens, in which he says that those who fought mask mandates are owed an "apology" — from whom, exactly, it is unclear. The CDC? Governors? Mayors? Hospital administrators? Anyone who wore one? Maybe all of the above.

It's true that recent studies have appeared to show little benefit from mask mandates in terms of reducing COVID's impact. Whether that unclear benefit comes from a lack of randomized trials, people's resistance to wearing masks even when required or improper mask-wearing — those things we may never know. But the point is both fair and taken: Mask mandates did not appear to do much to reduce COVID's spread.

Where I depart from the current GOP Monday Morning COVID-backing, though, is that those who recommended, created or even complied with mask mandates somehow owe an apology to those who opposed them.

I remember the early days of the pandemic, taking my boys to a playground to get them out of the house. It was eerily quiet on our walk there, and as they scampered over the slides and monkey bars, a man walking his dog approached and suggested (from a safe distance) that I take my kids home.

"The virus can live on the playground equipment for days," he told me, confidently.

Later, I tried to research his claim. But it soon became clear that the truth was discomforting — no one knew. It wasn't even clear at that point how the virus was transmitted. Was it through touch? Breathing? Saliva? We had yet to discover even the most basic details about the disease.

It would be some time before my kids would again touch playground equipment, though eventually we decided the risk of avoiding outdoor play was low enough and the cost high enough to take the chance.

We all made similar calculations in those early days. What was the risk versus reward of cleaning your groceries? Wearing a mask while outside? Going into the office?

We did the best we could.

The same, I think it should be emphasized, went for public officials, doctors and scientists and public policy experts and politicians, the people who had to recommend and make rules for managing the pandemic.

We made — they made — in some cases, the wrong call.

But with mask mandates, the pandemic's massive risk didn't have to do much to outweigh the minor reward of buying milk with your face uncovered. No adult was harmed by having to wear a face mask, and the questionable impact on children's development was balanced by a very understandable desire to prevent the deaths of millions of people.

When you know better, you do better, as the saying goes. But just as I don't believe I owe my children an apology for keeping them off the swing sets at the park, I don't believe the CDC owes anyone an apology for recommending face masks.

It *is* time for a debate about the continuing use of mask mandates — though it may be impossible to conduct the kind of trials necessary to prove whether masking prevents the transmission of COVID or other respiratory illnesses. And that debate should be informed by the best science we can find, but also by the understanding that true clarity on the topic is ephemeral, hard to grasp and illusory.

Doubt anyone who claims to know everything. Doubt anything that claims to explain it all.

Believe, only, that humans are all fallible and that we all fall short of perfection.

And we should, ultimately, expect only as much grace in our imperfections as we dispense.

Seasons' Greetings

2020 Has Been a Tough Year. If It Makes You Feel Better, It Could Be, and Has Been, Worse.

November 23, 2020

    Hello and welcome to the Holiday Calendar Year Support Group. This is our special Thanksgiving meeting, which, due to the coronavirus pandemic, we're holding over Zoom. Please keep all of your comments on-topic, keep them clean and keep them kind. And remember, no crosstalk. Now, 1933, would you like to start?

    1933: Yes, thanks. I have a few -

    2020: Excuse me. I hate to interrupt, 1933, but I've had a really rough time this year and my therapist says I need to get better about meeting my own emotional needs, so I'd like to go first.

    1933: I don't know what a 'therapist' is. I assume you meant 'bartender.'

    2020: I have been drinking more, yes, but, honestly, I haven't seen a bartender in almost nine months.

    1933: That sounds stressful. Try not seeing one for 13 years some time.

    2020: At least you didn't have to deal with a pandemic.

    1918: Um ...

    2020: Anyway, back to me. This year, our president was impeached, he lost the election and now he's angling to squat in the White House until federal marshals can manage to push past

Mitch McConnell guarding the doors of the Oval Office dining room, brush off the Burger King wrappers and empty Diet Coke cans and physically drag him out.

1941: Could be worse.

1933: Bet you didn't know that in my year, a group of millionaires plotted a coup to overthrow FDR and install a fascist dictator! It was Smedley Darlington Butler, 'Old Gimlet Eye,' they used to call him, back in thirty-trey -

1994: That is not a real name.

1933: Hush up, whippersnapper. Here's a peppermint, now go listen to some of your music CDs. What are you youngins into these days? Ace of Base?

1994: Only SOME OF US. The really cool people are all listening to Hole, not showering and wearing unisex cologne.

1933: In my year, one out of every four people was unemployed.

1349: In my year, half of a continent died.

1978: ZOOM BOMB! Hey-o, it's New Year's Eve here in 1978! Nixon's gone, "Animal House" just got released, gas is 60 cents a gallon and cellphones are roughly the size and weight of a jumbo modular brick! No Instagram for us, baby! Whoo hoo! <Click>

2020: Anyway, back to me. We've also had a lot of tragic deaths, protests and police brutality.

1968: Please, tell me more.

2020: I'm feeling very triggered by this one-upsmanship. At least your holidays weren't canceled. You still got together on Thanksgiving, Christmas. We're just sitting here, waiting for a vaccine -

1349: A vaccine? You mean, you have something better than leeches?

2020: I mean, we will. But we're going to have to wait months. Months of no play dates, no concerts, no movies. And sports is really lame without fans!

1943: I hate to keep bringing it back to us World War II years, but so many of our baseball players went to fight in the war, they considered canceling professional baseball.

1994: Suuure you hate to keep bringing it back to yourself.

1968: What are you even doing here, 1994?

1994: I think I'm energized by all the negativity and depression. Plus, I like the nostalgia.

1349: You have nostalgia for 1968? What is wrong with you?

1994: I had Boomers for parents.

1952: I heard that! I was upstairs on my Glenn Miller fan club Zoom call, but I still heard that! You do realize that my year was the absolute nadir of American cookery, right? Do you want me to make my famous ham-and-cream-of-cauliflower Jell-O for Thanksgiving dinner again?

1994: Please don't.

2020: All this arguing is starting to make me really miss Thanksgiving dinner with my family, when we spend 20 minutes debating how to carve the turkey. Then my aunt says we shouldn't put the football game on because of CTE and the shameful way Colin Kaepernick was treated, and then my grandpa says he agrees we shouldn't watch because those "flag-kneelers" are disrespecting the troops and then we have to sit there in front of Tucker Carlson's show until grandpa falls asleep on the couch and we can sneak the remote out of his hands to change the channel. Sigh.

1918: Look, it's time to wrap it up. And I think we can agree, things could always be better, but things could also always be a heckuva lot worse. Let's use this Thanksgiving as an opportunity to recognize the ways we have been blessed. Let's wear our masks, keep our distance, and get back together next year, when things will, we hope, be so much improved.

2024: Yeah, plus, might as well settle in for a while, because my year is gonna be a doozy.

(c) 2023 Pioneer Press. All rights reserved. Distributed by Tribune Content Agency, LLC.

Hope Can Be a Powerful Thing. Let's Gift Ourselves a Bit of It This Holiday Season.

November 30, 2020

Walking through my neighborhood the other day, I noticed how many of us have already decorated our houses this year. We've put up the Christmas lights, dragged the tree out of the basement and tacked up the wreath, calendars be damned.

It brought a tear to my eye, the indomitable cheer did, reminding me of my son's first Christmas present, the one I bought him before he was born, before he was conceived, actually, when he was nothing more than a tender shoot of hope blooming in my soul.

We'd been Trying (with a capital T) to have children for years, and Trying had made way for Increasingly More Invasive Ways of Trying, with nothing but failures and miscarriages dotting the landscape thus far.

Then one holiday season, I found myself in Colorado, about a half-mile from our IVF clinic, in a hotel waiting for my eggs to ripen enough to harvest. My husband was back in Chicago and though I worked remotely on the weekdays, I was otherwise aimless and lonely. I decided one weekend to take a day trip to The Stanley Hotel, the inspiration for Stephen King's Overlook Hotel in "The Shining," an appropriately grim pilgrimage.

I drove my rented car into the Rocky Mountains on a gray

Saturday afternoon, stopping halfway up to let a caravan of elk cross the highway in front of me. Once there, I walked the hotel's grounds, snapping pictures to text to my husband, as if to say, "See how much fun I'm having?"

Eventually, I wandered into the gift shop, decorated richly for Christmas with evergreen boughs and white lights. To that point, I'd stayed far away from any purchases that might hint at even the loosest belief that I would one day have a child. There were no tiny clothes, no baby books or cribs in our house. Our second bedroom prominently featured a giant easel and my acrylic paint set.

"I'm not living as if this is a baby's room," I'd say.

So it was with some trepidation, and a fair amount of shame, that I approached the kids' section of The Stanley Hotel's store.

I ran my hand along the wooden trains, holiday clothes and alighted on a small stuffed dog.

I picked it up, felt its soft cotton ears and knitted body. I turned over the price tag and winced. An absurd amount, I thought, for such a tiny toy, one only large enough to fit a newborn's arms. I put it back.

I picked out fridge magnets and Christmas tree ornaments, a T-shirt I thought my husband would like. I kept looking over, though, at the stuffed dog. I tentatively picked it up again, and again tsked at the price. Some nameless force, though, kept it in my hand.

I checked out, paid for it all and drove back to the hotel. I told no one, even my husband when he arrived in Denver. I pushed the toy into the bottom of my suitcase like a secret and took it home.

When I unpacked my bags, I took the stuffed dog out of its plastic bag. Without deciding to, and without understanding why, I wrapped it in thick, cream-colored wrapping paper decorated with holly. Around the outside of the package, I tied a red-and-gold ribbon. I made a tiny card, one you'd have to open to read, and inside wrote, in black lettering, "To Baby, from Mom and Dad."

Reading the words made me sick with pity for the person

who'd written them, for it was obviously not me. To claim the name "Mom" would have been delusional, and who was this non-existent Baby, anyway? I wasn't even pregnant, and there was no sign on the horizon of getting to that stage, itself no guarantee of parenthood, as I had learned through hard lessons.

Filled with shame, I tucked the wrapped present away in The Stanley Hotel plastic bag, and stuffed it deep in a shopping bag full of wrapping paper, one I shoved to the back of a knee wall cubbyhole.

I still didn't tell my husband, knew he would give me a sad look, one that I would have sorely earned, one that would have asked, "You're buying gifts for a baby we don't have?"

I ignored the present that Christmas, pretended to forget it even existed. When I took the bag of wrapping paper out the following Christmas, I was nearly two-thirds of the way through a terrifying, endangered pregnancy. I felt no more confident than I had the previous Christmas.

Then, I truly did forget about the present, for almost a year, in the bustle of freshly minted parenthood and Christmas planning and showing off our baby at family holiday parties.

I found the present when digging for gift labels. My hand closed around the soft package, then I pulled it out and gasped. I still didn't feel like that woman, Mom, on the label, but the boy cooing softly in the bassinet beside me proved me wrong. I was her. He was Baby. We were parents.

I realized then that the force that had compelled me to buy the stuffed dog, the same one since gnawed by the merciless gums of not one but two babies, was nothing more than hope.

Hope that refused to be shamed out of existence, hope that kept me returning to that clinic in Colorado, kept me jabbing myself with shots of hormones and kept me trekking through even much lower valleys, all for slim but powerful hope.

Now it's holiday season again, and I see the evidence of our collective hope around me. In the lights on our houses, the ones put up extra early this year, and the twinkle from the ornaments on our Christmas trees, there's that hope again.

We hope for hugs from grandmothers, time with our grandchildren, the return of our jobs, the reopening of our businesses. We hope that 2021 brings a reprieve from fear, from illness, from pain.

So, my hope for all of us is that we celebrate thoroughly this year, whatever we choose to celebrate, whether it be Christmas or Hanukkah or Kwanzaa or Winter Solstice or just the weary end of a very long year. Decorate. Bake the cookies, watch the movies, drink the eggnog. Buy the present.

Cover yourself in hope, this holiday season.

Take it from me: It will, some day, bring you the most amazing gifts.

(c) 2023 Pioneer Press. All rights reserved. Distributed by Tribune Content Agency, LLC.

Halloween Ghouls Have Nothing On Potty Training

October 23, 2021

It'll be Halloween soon — prime time for scary movie fans.

Some are into "The Shining," the story of a man who goes crazy from spending too much time alone with his family without alcohol. Others prefer "Friday The 13th," a movie that teaches us that the top risk factor for becoming a serial killer's victim is premarital sex.

Me, though? I don't need horror movies, for I have recently potty trained a 3-year-old.

Before I begin, a content advisory: What follows is parental gore. It's nasty, offensive and, unless you've been thoroughly desensitized, tough to tolerate.

The first thing you should know about potty training a 3-year-old is that it's already too late.

That, at least, is the perspective you'll find in the most popular potty training book, one that's long on shame and short on understanding.

You'll read the book anyway, though, through gritted teeth if necessary. Because you're trying to turn your child from someone who saunters up, with the casual ease of a kid hauling two pounds of poop in his shorts, to demand a diaper change into a person who can use the bathroom independently.

It's a transformation on par with a caterpillar becoming a butterfly: It's messy, slow and mysterious but somehow, someway, the job gets done.

Speaking of jobs, yours, as a potty-training parent, is to bribe.

Act like you're bidding for a massive city contract; if you want to make it happen, you better stuff your ethics in a sack.

This is no time for petty moralities, questions about "what kind of message you're sending" or considerations of three months from now, when your child will demand M&Ms for every bowel movement. You're setting a potty trap, one baited with candy, toys and stickers.

The next step is cultivating an ecstatic response to the smells, sights and sounds of toileting.

"Wow!"

"Yay!"

"Awesome!"

These are not words you will have previously associated with feces. That will change.

You should also prepare yourself for the inevitable and understandable disgust with which nonparents will treat the subject. It may be hard for you to remember how it feels not to be waiting, day in and day out, with decreasing patience and increasing desperation, for someone to poop.

But the vast majority of your childless friends and relatives won't enjoy hearing about the exact color, size and consistency of your offspring's excrement. When your kid insists on FaceTiming someone to show them the contents of the family toilet, Grandma's your best bet.

I also suggest you get ready for a lot of al fresco peeing. Whether you're at the park, riding bikes around the neighborhood or walking out of the grocery store, you must be prepared to immediately stop and search frantically for a bush or tree to serve as cover. Don't forget to keep an eye out for witnesses. I don't *think* you'd get arrested merely for allowing some light public urination, but you're certainly in danger of getting disapproving glares.

Ultimately, there are many scary and disturbing parts to potty training, among them the risk that you will one day announce to a room full of adults that you "need to go potty."

But worst of all is that, at some point, months or even years in the future, when you're sorting through unused diapers and deciding whether to get rid of the changing table, you might actually start to miss it: the diaper bags and the wipes and the accoutrements of infancy.

You'll get sad.

Because having a baby who doesn't wear diapers means he's not quite a baby anymore.

And that feels crappy.

A Gift Worth Giving Thanks For

November 20, 2021

Whenever my parents would ask us kids at the Thanksgiving dinner table to report on what we were grateful for, I'd roll my eyes so hard I practically fell over.

How cheesy.

But, as with licking your finger to wipe smudges from your kid's face or justifying things with "because I said so," often we find ourselves returning to the script our own parents wrote.

Therefore, this year, I'm making a Thanksgiving gratitude list, and near the top is a gift I got from a dead person: a knee ligament.

I had surgery recently — the repair of an old injury — and I'm still recovering. Everyone who sees me limping or who saw my brace asks how I did it.

I usually deliver a version of the truth, a "tore my ACL" or "fell down." The full story's too embarrassing; it makes me want to melt into the ground like a popsicle in July.

I hurt it breaking up a fight at a house party.

Whose house? No clue.

The combatants? Had never met them before, have never encountered them since.

Were they drunk? Stinking.

Why did I try to get between two strange, inebriated men? Your guess is as good as mine.

I mean, I've always been an interfering person, the kind who can't help but weigh in. Once, I heard a chiropractor tell his patient that if he thought he was having a heart attack, he should take cayenne pepper instead of calling 911.

"Take the cayenne pepper, if you want," I blurted out, "but call 911, too."

That cost me a half-hour of my life, which was spent arguing with the chiropractor and his wife, and ended only when I agreed to accept 20 pages printed out from Yahoo answers.

But back to the knee.

Ever since my ill-advised attempt at conflict resolution, my knee has given out sporadically, when I twisted it, slipped or just stepped wrong. It got particularly bad earlier this year, leaving me incapable of walking to the playground with my kids or achieving even my normally poor golf performance.

A surgeon told me he could graft a cadaver ligament onto my knee to replace the one I'd been living without for so many years. The surgery promised a long, slow recovery, with only the hope of increased stability.

In the months since, it's been steadily improving. I used to say I only ran when chased, but last week, I found myself jogging on the treadmill, something I hadn't dared since the advent of the smartphone.

And I've thought a lot about the donor whose ligament I now use. I don't know the person's age or gender, have no clue what their life was like or how they died.

But I wonder what my donated ligament did before it found its way into my knee.

Did it run for the train to avoid being late for an awesome first job? Did it swing on monkey bars and jump off into the waiting arms of a loving mom?

I'll never know, and perhaps that's for the best.

My knee has a past, but it also has new tasks, new hills, both literal and figurative, to climb.

It's helping me play trains with my kids and take long walks to the park. It's giving me gifts, every day, in a thousand small ways.

So, when I make my list this Thanksgiving, I'll make sure to mention that mysterious, wonderful gift, given in grief but received as a blessing, from another person's body into my own.

The gift not of life, in my case, but of a better one.

A gift worth the thanksgiving.

The Joy of Christmas, Surpassed Only by the Joy of Christmas Past

December 18, 2021

Every day for what feels like the last two months, my 3-year-old has asked me the same question:

"Is today Christmas?"

He asks in a voice mixed with both excitement and dread, full of the expectation of a thrilling day but also the fear that, when it finally arrives, something may be required of him for which he's not entirely prepared.

Honestly, his attitude, a frappe of anticipation and anxiety, mirrors my own.

Pre-parenthood, the idea of holidays with kids was gentle, full of nostalgia for the sweet parts of my own childhood and amnesia for the harsher times. What I've realized as a parent is that the most common Christmas experience is bone-deep exhaustion.

It's list-making and planning, cooking and baking, gift-seeking and gift-buying — to say nothing of the wrapping. Then, there's the real grind: the constant, unremitting lying.

There are the fibs about Santa, of course, the invention of an entire backstory for whatever kind of person would move to a barren wasteland to live out his days in the company of several hundred tiny creatures just as strange as he is, toiling ceaselessly in the hopes of meeting, if only for one day, the material demands of billions of bratty kids.

There are the lies about the letters and how they arrive, the elves and the reindeer, the Grinch, Frosty the Snowman — by the time you're done, you've sewn a virtual quilt of fabrications.

"Do the elves ever die?"

"Can Santa see what I'm doing at Grandma's?"

"Does he eat cookies at every house?"

It's exhausting, frankly, and makes you realize how easily you'd crack under police interrogation.

This year, I also set myself a series of further obstacles to serenity: I decided to handmake presents and bake homemade treats.

"Fruitcake!" I thought a month ago. "What a great idea!"

When I found myself, a few weeks later, elbow-deep in pounds of dried fruit, the promise of weeks of tending to the cake with freshly sherried cheesecloth standing in front of me, the idea seemed mysteriously dumb — bizarre even.

"Who set this pointless task for me?" I asked myself, knowing full well that the answer was Pre-Holiday Me, a starry-eyed idiot.

Pre-Holiday Me also planned to make hot chocolate mix by hand, stuff it into tiny glass containers and cover them in squares of red tartan cloth cut by hand, tied with a jute-ribbon bow.

"How festive!" Pre-Holiday me thought. "How adorable!"

Holiday Me found the experience slightly less adorable as I peered through my reading glasses at the tiny tags I'd bought, my hands cramping as I wrote words small enough to make an ant squint.

Meanwhile, the demands of everyday life do not — no matter how much I might wish — pause, even for a second.

In a religion class years ago, I learned about the Buddhist concept of "samsara," the endless, miserable cycle of death and rebirth to which all nonenlightened humans are fated to endure.

Laundry, in other words.

It all sounds rather pathetic, and I know that it both could be and, for many people, is far worse. I'm cringing as I complain about having too much family, too many presents, too much food.

Still, I can't help but think of our toddler's conflicted holiday spirit.

When we ask him what he wants for Christmas, he mulls it over with a kind of confused wonder, marveling at the possibilities but also the peril.

"Nothing," he seems to say. "Everything."

Somehow, he already knows it's a mixed bag.

When the holiday finally comes, I expect that it will be with his mixture of relief and sadness that I answer him: "Yes, honey, today is Christmas. Thank God."

The Christmas Truce of 1914 Remains a Miracle and an Inspiration

December 25, 2021

Nearly 107 years later, the events of Dec. 25, 1914, commonly known as the Christmas truce, remain mystical, remarkable — but most of all, instructive.

The Great War had only begun in July, but by the Christmas season, the soldiers were tired of battle and likely had expected to be home already.

Many of the fighting men hailed from small European villages, where cars and even electric lights were new arrivals. The scale of the suffering those naive combatants had seen in four short months would be, to modern minds, unimaginable, with 27,000 French soldiers dying in just one bleak August day.

They'd recently been introduced to both chemical weapons and trench warfare, with its concomitant degradations of filth, vermin and disease.

Soaking wet in the muddy trenches they'd dug as "temporary" structures, the denizens of the front line spent the weeks leading up to Christmas bitten by rats, malnourished from disruptions in their supply deliveries and surrounded by the decaying bodies of their comrades.

A traumatized Ernest Hemingway, who as a teenager had driven an ambulance during the war, would later write, "Never think that war, no matter how necessary, nor how justified, is not a crime."

Pope Benedict XV had written to the leaders of the warring nations asking for a cessation in hostilities for Christmas, a request that had been denied. Superiors threatened and admonished men who considered laying down their arms.

And they couldn't have thought well of each other.

German schoolchildren were taught a poem that extolled the values of hating the British, and Rudyard Kipling wrote this in a London newspaper:

"However the world pretends to divide itself, there are only two divisions in the world today — human beings and Germans."

The stakes couldn't have been higher, for even death itself was a risk. The combatants had no guarantees that an overture wouldn't be rebuffed, that they wouldn't be greeted with bullets instead of holiday cheer.

But when Christmas Eve came, the sounds of "Stille Nacht" floated across the frozen No Man's Land.

By the next day, some soldiers were trading whiskey and cigarettes, chatting with one another in broken English and German, maybe even playing friendly games of soccer (if the apocryphal accounts were true).

The respite was brief. Soon, the men had returned to fighting.

But for that one Christmas Day, something had taken place that has not been repeated since. The truce wasn't sanctioned by higher offices, wasn't planned or encouraged.

The men overcame their biases, their direct orders, their fear of death. They overcame their exhaustion and hunger, their deprivation and their distrust.

Soldiers celebrated and sang, played children's games where dead bodies had lain. They ignored their empty bellies and used their rations as presents, handing over their cigars and candy to men who were trying to kill them.

The charity of the rich is weak, for those who have too much give only what they cannot use. The charity of the deprived holds divine power.

The Christmas truce was a miracle of biblical proportions.

We are not, in 2021, fighting one another with tanks and machine guns, but we battle all the same. Our spirits are broken from years of disease, and our biases have been inflamed by the propaganda of war.

We have been made small.

But as the men of the Western Front in 1914 have shown us, none are so small that they might not grow.

We can throw off the chains of our ill will and our sadness. We can rise above, defy our leaders and reach a hand across No Man's Land.

We can be good to one another, if only for one Christmas Day, if only we might try.

Springtime Brings a Blooming Bouquet — of Illness

March 26, 2022

After two long years of winter, it's finally starting to feel like spring.

Because, at least in our house, we're entering our third straight week of one or more family members being sick with an ever-rotating type of non-COVID illness.

In the Before Times, preschools, parties and playdates were giant virus incubators, kids jostling to be the first to transmit their runny noses and hacking coughs to the rest of the crew.

The winter of 2019-2020, our younger son was sick, in an unbroken streak, for months, coming down with stomach flus, colds and croups. We made not one but two trips to the ER the week of Christmas, one on Christmas Day itself, with sick kids.

But in March of 2020, the coughing stopped. There were no more runny noses or fevers. No one woke up puking in the middle of the night. Kids forgot the taste of children's Tylenol and grape Pedialyte.

Due to quarantines, masking and social distancing, our children have been silently, eerily well.

We parents have forgotten those times, too.

"They're going to be sick for months," I warned my husband when the masks started coming off at schools and daycares.

The "sick season" was bad pre-COVID, but now there's their stunted immune systems to deal with. Without practice, their little bodies have developed all the immunological defenses of a wet paper towel.

Our grown-up bodies are similarly weakened.

The other day, I found myself, sick with a cold and nostrils completely blocked, walking my kid toward school when I realized I had a problem.

I had no Kleenex, and one of two things was about to happen: I was either going to choke to death on a giant globule of post-nasal drip or I was going to spit out a snot-blob in front of my son's entire kindergarten class.

I turned my head, discreetly, and made like a catcher during spring training.

When I looked back, I saw the dad of one of my son's best friends smiling at me and waving. His hand halted, mid-air, and a look passed across his face, a questioning look that seemed to be saying,

"Did she just ... hock a loogie?"

I played it off.

Hahaha, nothing to see here! my answering smile said with confidence. *I would never do something that disgusting!*

I'm already borderline with the folks at this school after I had to let my younger son pee on the majestic tree in the kindergarten playground after school one day.

"I need to go," he said, holding the front of his pants and giving me *the look,* the look all parents of a potty-trained-or-training kid know, the look that says:

If we don't get to a bathroom in 30 seconds, you're going to have a lot of cleaning to do.

"Can you wait?" I asked, already knowing the answer.

"No," he said, firmly.

So, I did what any parent would do, which is "let your kid pee on a tree while you try to melt into the sidewalk."

I mean, COVID quarantines are horrible, but, as with winters, there are some benefits.

Back in the long pandemic winter, during the days of outside masking, I could have credibly denied being the person who let her kid publicly water the school oak tree. And instead of worrying about spitting in public, I could have performed some privately humiliating but face-saving maneuver with my mask.

On balance, though, I think I'll stick with spring.

After all, embarrassment fades, kids get over colds and parents forget seeing other parents' kids peeing on trees.

At least, I hope they do.

Summer's Table Holds Delights Too Many To Count

June 11, 2022

When summer approaches, some diet, hoping to get their bodies swimsuit-ready. Me? I'm getting my stomach prepared for summer food.

Winter might offer soup, casseroles and chili, but it can't hold a candle to summer's riot of tastes.

From appetizers to dessert, summer's got it all. There are drinks — iced tea, sweetened or black, and cold beer after a sweaty day of work. There are popsicles eaten on porches and cheeseburgers, swollen and juicy, served on paper plates laden with potato salad.

Second only to Thanksgiving and Christmas, there's no other season when food is so much at the forefront of all we do.

In any case, you can make pumpkin pie any day of the week, any week of the year, but there's only a brief, luxurious window where you can get a perfect, deep-pink watermelon.

Every summer, I try to grow food. In the past, I've mostly limited my efforts to herbs like basil and oregano. The only thing I've successfully been able to coax back year after year has been my chives. This year, mysteriously, chamomile has started popping up across our lawn like a weed.

I'm too much of a city slicker to confidently eat wild food, but just the smell is enough to transport me, back in time and thousands of miles away, to my childhood in Greece, where chamomile and fennel lined the sides of the dusty streets.

A couple of days ago, I took my younger son to the gardening shop to look for plants for a food garden.

A mother bunny has built a burrow in our backyard and though she seems to be poaching our greenery for her babies, they're too cute to resent. Instead, I suggested we buy plants the rabbits wouldn't like.

We picked out mild banana peppers and a hot Hungarian wax pepper plant. They joined a cucumber sprout my older son had been tending, and a few seeds he'd collected and nurtured inside. What we were really trying to grow, though, was memories.

Many of my own best childhood memories revolve around summer food. I think of summers past and remember ripe apricots, plucked from the trees in my grandparents' orchard, and tomatoes, blood-red and juicy, drowned in olive oil and dusted with salt.

I remember using paring knives to wedge limpets off rocks at the ocean's edge, squeezing lemon juice on top and eating them raw. There was octopus caught fresh from the sea, my grandfather slinging it against the concrete walls of our beach shack to soften it for roasting.

I remember the smell of fire-grilled meat at dusk, pork souvlaki cooked at tavernas in the village center. Our parents would let us stay up late, playing in the street, until the food was ready, and we ate it in groups, our families and friends around us in a summer feast.

Different parts of the country have their own specific summer foods — especially fruits and vegetables we wait all year to enjoy. Here in the Midwest, we have fat Michigan blueberries, Door County cherries and corn so sweet you don't even have to cook it.

I imagine where you live, there are your own summer treats, but there are some experiences most of us share.

I hope you've heard the trill of an ice cream truck, dropped whatever toy you were holding and stopped whatever game you were playing to chase the sound, so specifically summery and so joyous.

There's no culinary joy like the joy of summer eating.

And this year, I hope you enjoy every delight summer's plate has to offer. I plan to.

In fact, if you'll excuse me, my stomach's grumbling right now. I think I'll go make myself a snack.

What Am I Thankful For? Don't Make Me Say It

November 19, 2022

I love Thanksgiving and its traditions — the homemade centerpieces, the bad football, the interminable televised parades — but there's one I'd rather skip.

It's an almost-inescapable tradition, one that usually rears its head just as you're sitting down to eat. Everyone's starving because the turkey took forever to cook, and plates loaded with cranberries and pumpkin pie waft delicious smells your way.

As you reach to grab your fork, Aunt Gladys speaks up.

"Wait," she says, holding up her hand. "First let's all go around the table and say what we're thankful for."

As an adult, I push aside my annoyance and summon up an answer: family, health, friends. It never feels particularly genuine, but the job's done. When I was a child, though, that kind of gratitude-on-demand infuriated me, made me want to do what my toddler did last year and snap back:

Nothing. I'm thankful for nothing.

Lest you think I'm simply a curmudgeon, let me reassure you: I know the importance of gratitude.

I personally have felt its power. When I was pregnant with my older son, I was confined to bed for months. I was isolated, scared and stressed. Making gratitude lists prevented me from living too far in the future, kept me grounded in the present.

I used to ask myself: What am I grateful for today? Sometimes it was just a new episode of "The Great British Baking Show" or a nice bowl of tomato soup delivered by my mother-in-law. But whatever it was, however small, thinking about it helped.

And gratitude doesn't just work for me: Study after study has shown that having gratitude can improve your mental and physical health, your outlook on life and even your performance at certain tasks.

Cicero called gratitude the "parent" of all other virtues.

Gratitude *is* great.

So why is it so annoying when someone demands us to be grateful?

Maybe because gratitude is a journey without a destination. There are times we feel more grateful, and less, and at one point, we may be just as likely to feel petty as we are gracious.

The same way that you can't make yourself fall in love, you cannot manufacture gratitude.

We might feel a wave of gratitude watching our kids pick up their plates after dinner and put them in the dishwasher. Or maybe we'll sit, with a full belly, in front of the TV later that night and sigh in bliss.

When gratitude flies by like that, we should grab it, quickly, before it disappears.

Right now, we might think, *I feel lucky.*

But false gratitude is worse than none.

God instructed the faithful to pray behind closed doors instead of in public, like hypocrites. Similarly, the act of performing gratitude cheapens it, somewhat.

A University of California, Berkeley paper on the "science of gratitude" listed some of the barriers to gratitude, among them "envy, materialism, narcissism, and cynicism."

When we post extended thankfulness peans on Facebook, or announce our gratitude to a table of Thanksgiving guests, that moment is, bizarrely, all about us. And when we're caught up in ourselves, the expression of gratitude can become fake, superficial.

    I've decided instead this year to express my gratitude organically, hopefully to the very person who's boosted me up. I recently wrote a letter to a woman I'd never met, thanking her for a speech she gave decades ago.

    I hope that, in a way, the letter, and whatever other in-the-moment gratitude I find, will make up for my uninspiring performance at the dinner table, when Aunt Gladys demands I stand and deliver.

    For even though sincerity is ideal, there's nothing wrong with phoning it in from time to time, either.

    After all, that pumpkin pie won't eat itself. And for that, I'm thankful.

Christmas: The Season of Lying

December 3, 2022

When the stockings are hung by the chimney with care, lies about St. Nicholas soon will be there.

For though the Yuletide means a great many things to a great many people, to me, it mostly means preparing myself to deceive.

It's the season of giving for some, but, for me, it's the season of lying.

In every other aspect of my parenting, I try to cultivate trust with my children. Whether they're asking about death or about poop, I work hard to be honest, in the most age-appropriate way possible.

The other day, my older son asked me to explain, in detail, how sperm gets into a woman's body. I did my best to give him a G-rated yet accurate accounting, knowing that I neither want to completely spoil his innocence nor provide content so explicit that he can't safely repeat it at school. I told the truth, gently but completely.

Contrast that to our recent conversations about Santa, during which I do nothing other than lob falsehoods his way.

"Will we see Santa this year?"

"Of course. We'll see him at the mall."

"Why does he go to the mall?"

"To, um, find out what kids want for Christmas."

"How does he remember all of that?"

"He ... has a really good memory."

"Have I met Santa before?"

"Uh, yes, we went to the mall a few years ago."

"Will he know my name?"

"I don't think so."

"But you said he had a really good memory."

The kids want to know why Santa doesn't give grown-ups presents. They want to know what gets you on the naughty list and whether those on it really get coal for Christmas. They want to know whether Santa ever gets sick of cookies.

I'm sure that the older one will notice that the Mall Santa looks a little different than the Tree-Lighting Santa and even more different than Thanksgiving Day Parade Santa.

I don't know what I'll say in explanation, but whatever it is, it will be a lie.

So I lie about Santa, I lie about our chimney and the North Pole and the Polar Express train and the elves.

Boy, do I lie about the elves.

I lie about the Elf on the Shelf, that fiendish invention, and why he looks like a doll but is actually a magical creature capable of seeing through walls and hearing conversations held on other floors of the house.

"Why doesn't Smokey Choo-Choo move when I can see him?" (Our elf was christened Smokey Choo-Choo several years ago and though they've tried to change his name, the new one never sticks.)

"The book says Santa told him not to move when we can see him."

"Why? That's mean. He needs to stretch his legs."

(I agree, kid, that would be cruel, if Smokey Choo-Choo were anything other than a bolt of fabric stuffed with polyester filling.)

Why is the Elf on the Shelf so small? Why do his eyes always look to the side, as if he were caught in the middle of some illegal activity? When does Smokey Choo-Choo sleep, and where on Earth does he poop?

After all this lying, I can do nothing other than hang my head in shame.

If there were a naughty list, I'd deserve to be on it.

One day, I'll have to stop all the Christmas lying and figure out a way to explain myself. But not today. Not this year. Not now.

Because while I still have the chance, I'll relish the tales of Santa, of magic, of complex Christmas miracles.

It's not a lie, after all, if you believe it, too.

The First, and Only, Honest Christmas Cookie Recipe

December 24, 2022

This is an honest Christmas cookie recipe.

Current fashion in online recipes is to begin by treating readers to a personal essay about the emotional impact almonds have had on your life, followed by a culinary genealogy of cookies, stretching back to William the Conqueror.

But I've got 354 presents to wrap, so let's get going.

Ingredients:

Butter, brought to room temperature. On the countertop, this takes between three hours and four days. Or microwave it and accidentally create butter soup. Your call.

Flour. You likely have a bag left over from the Great Bread-Making Era of the Pandemic. Expiration date: July 2021. I'm sure it's fine, though.

Slivered (not chopped) raw (not roasted) almonds. They're in the baking aisle. Or the snack aisle. Or the candy aisle or the seasonal aisle. Or maybe an end cap with the fruitcake ingredients, conveniently placed for the three people in the world who still make fruitcake.

Powdered sugar. How much? Well, when you sneeze, your kitchen's going to look like Pablo Escobar's bathroom.

1/16 tsp of an exotic ingredient requiring four grocery

store trips and a final, desperate drive across town to a specialty shop where the proprietor has blue hair, smells like patchouli and wears a T-shirt reading, "Ask me about my podcast."

Now you're ready to bake!

Directions:

1. Gather the kids and excitedly inform them of the upcoming magical holiday experience. When you tell them what kind of cookies you're making, listen, with a tight smile, as they tell you that they "hate almonds" and won't eat those cookies, never EVER. Remind them that an hour earlier, they were eating almonds you needed for the recipe and saying, "Yum! Almonds!"

2. Beat the eggs, which are at room temperature. If the eggs are cold, have the kids watch a little TV while they warm up.

3. Two hours later, when the kids refuse to get up from the couch, make the cookies by yourself, resentfully.

4. Slowly add the sugar to the beaten eggs. Slower than that! SLOWER! OK, now that's too slow. Speed it up. Oops. It all fell in, didn't it?

5. Add the rest of the ingredients with your youngest child, who wanders in and asks to help. Realize after he dips his hand into the dough and starts licking it off his fingers that he hasn't washed his hands. Consider that he also probably just got salmonella from the raw eggs.

6. Use an ice cream scooper to perfectly portion 1/4 cup of dough. When you can't find the ice cream scooper, use a spoon. Resign yourself to the fact that some will be the size of a baseball and others the size of a marble.

7. Take the cookies to the preheated oven.

8. Notice that you forgot to preheat the oven.

9. Bake the cookies at 350 degrees for 10 minutes, unless it's a nonstick tray, in which case it's 325 degrees for 12 minutes, unless it's a convection oven, in which case it's 375 for 5 minutes, unless you live in a high-altitude area, in which case just go to the grocery store and buy premade cookies because no one's going to know the difference anyway.

10. Yell at the kids that they better get in here if they want

to frost the cookies.

11. Try, and fail, to prevent them eating 37 cookies apiece during decorating.

12. Give the youngest one the blue frosting. Now the green. WAIT, no, the red. Actually, the blue. Can the oldest have some sprinkles? Not those sprinkles, the ones in the pantry.

13. Obsequiously praise the artistry on the cookies, even the ones that look like the dog might have puked them up. Especially those.

14. Excuse the kids to watch more TV.

15. Eat 10 cookies, one at a time, each time promising that this is *absolutely* the last one.

16. Now, congratulate yourself on a job well done and have a nice glass of wine. Or two. The holidays are hard, and you deserve it.

Midwestern Weather: The Worst, Other Than Everywhere Else

March 11, 2023

It's a cold March day in the Midwest, with fresh-fallen snow on the ground, and this is about the time every year when I consider grabbing the family and absconding to some southern climate, escaping like a thief in the night to any place you don't have to have to wear snowshoes on spring break.

Yes, the winter weather (and sometimes the fall weather and usually the spring weather) is terrible in the Midwest.

The air whips in over our 10 million lakes, and the closer you are to the water, the worse it gets. In Midwestern cities, tall buildings create icy wind tunnels, and sometimes, it doesn't matter how much thermal underwear you're wearing, you still eventually become certain that hell must not be hot but Minnesota-in-January cold.

"But, the summer!" Midwesterners remind ourselves, thinking about how we blossom in the sun, shedding our puffy coats and crowding into farmers markets. There's a solid two months where the weather's perfect in the Midwest, and we experience the same kind of forgetfulness that causes women to have more than one baby and people to sign up for multiyear gym memberships.

In the long winter, though, Midwesterners reconsider our choices. We have longing thoughts, reveries, about other places in the U.S.

Should we move to California, Louisiana, Florida, Colorado,

Arizona — places where people look down on our weather with a mixture of pity and schadenfreude?

Well, I'm here to tell you, no. Don't do it. They may not have the punishing Midwestern winters, but their weather has its flaws, too. Envy them not, cold-weather denizens.

In California, you've got droughts and mudslides and earthquakes and fires — biblical meteorological events that seem to come as punishment both for being spoiled the rest of the year and for giving rise to an ever-increasing supply of Kardashians. There's a permanent haze of smog over Los Angeles, and the water at a Pacific Ocean beach is as icy as Lake Michigan in spring.

True, the only things icy about Arizona are their attitudes toward Democrats, but the weather there is no great shakes, either. The entire state shimmers in the heat like an empty Walmart parking lot, waves of radiant energy rising from the pavement. It's so hot in Arizona, opening your front door is like opening a convection oven. Virginia may be for lovers, but Arizona is for lizards.

Now, when it comes to ovens, the chefs in New Orleans certainly operate theirs with uncommon skill, but the sticky weather there wins no prizes. The air in the city is as heavy as a crawfish etouffee, and the clouds just kind of give up every day around 2 p.m. and release the excess moisture as rain. You know who likes the weather in New Orleans? Cockroaches. It's their Key West.

Speaking of Florida, I must admit, the state does perform a nifty trick, combining Arizona's heat with New Orleans' humidity in a climate only an alligator could love. Air conditioning is your only weapon. My Greek grandmother thought air conditioning made you sick, something I never believed until I walked into a Florida store and felt the sweat on my arms instantly freeze in protest.

The only place I've been with truly enviable weather is Colorado. It's warm in the summer and, thanks to the high altitude and low humidity, the winters don't feel as punishing. True, you need a graphing calculator to determine recipe cooking times and you walk everywhere through a fog of marijuana smoke, but that's a small price to pay for getting both snow on Christmas and swimming pools in the summer.

But you know what? Like most Midwesterners, I'm not going anywhere, even to Colorado. Because, really, we don't live here for the weather. We live here for the friendly people, the fatty food and the way the rest of the country forgets we exist.

We may hate the cold, but that just makes us ever more resistant to letting it defeat us.

Plus, it's nice here, even when you're shoveling the sidewalk in April.

That's what I'm telling myself, anyway.

The Days Go Slowly

Camping Is Not for Me: A Diatribe

June 7, 2021

My son wants to go camping.

I, on the other hand, would rather have all of my teeth pulled out, slowly, one-by-one, sans anesthesia, by a guy who does dentistry in his spare time, using antique tools he bought on eBay.

As you can see, we're at a bit of an impasse.

I went camping once, with a friend from high school and her parents. I was 15, and the only thing I learned was that if it's raining, and you touch the walls of the tent where you're freezing your buns off, water seeps through and soaks your lumpy little sleeping bag, too.

In the car ride home, my friend's mom told me to check my scalp for ticks.

"*TICKS*?!?" I squealed, raking my hands through my hair frantically. When an ugly little bug tumbled out, I screamed and tried to squish it.

Do you know that ticks are almost impossible to crush? They're bloodsucking, impenetrable tanks and they're only one of the offensive creatures you might encounter in the woods.

It was after that first, and last, camping trip that I realized: Many people love camping, and they are certainly welcome to it, but it's not for me.

Whenever I'm tempted, I ask myself why I would give up, for any length of time, running water, electricity, air conditioning - in short, some of the greatest advancements in the science of comfort? Why would I choose to subsist on granola and peanuts, like a squirrel? Why would I voluntarily put myself into a situation where I need to hide even that grim fare from marauding bears?

Then I think: You know who loved not having electricity? The Unabomber, that's who.

Now, lest you think I'm being snobby, no, it's not that I think I'm better than people who love camping. Maybe I'm worse. I'm certainly different.

A couple of years ago, someone suggested running to me as exercise. I told her what I tell everyone who mentions the sport:

"I only run when chased."

I covered the Chicago Marathon once for the Tribune and watching the back-of-the-packers cross the finish line, misery etched in every inch of their sweaty faces, I thought to myself, "Why would they do that to themselves, when they could watch the Food Network while they use the elliptical at the gym, then hop in the steam room, shower and grab a protein shake on the way out?"

Sometimes, when my husband and I are talking about farmers or dwellers of rural parts of the state, we'll express satisfaction with our suburban lives. He'll call himself a "city mouse," and a thrill will go through me, a voice whispering in my head, *you made the right decision.*

I have trouble picturing the reaction of my grandmother, who worked herself ill in the fields as a subsistence farmer, if I told her I was going to take a vacation that involved sleeping on dirt and squatting down to cook over an open flame.

Though, who knows, maybe she'd get it. She did, after all, spend most of her life washing clothes by hand, first heating up the water in a giant cast-iron caldron and then scrubbing the stains out on a washboard. When, in her old age, her sons bought her a washing machine, it sat unused in the bathroom, serving as a shelf for towels.

The washing machine never got the clothes clean enough, she told me.

"What about 'glamping'?" you ask. Or maybe you're asking, "What on earth is 'glamping'?"

Take it away, Glamping.com: "Glamping is where stunning nature meets modern luxury. It's a way to experience the untamed and completely unique parts of the world - without having to sacrifice creature comforts."

All the enlightenment without any of the suffering! And all it costs is a boatload of money.

Anyway, I experience the outside world. I love reading about mountain-climbing. One of my favorite books, in fact, is "Into Thin Air," the story of a tragedy that unfolded on Mount Everest in 1996. I lie in bed, cuddled up under the covers and sipping chamomile tea, wondering at the kind of people who find it fun to risk dying.

I'm sure there will be a time in my sons' lives where I will happily exchange indoor plumbing for the opportunity to talk to them without the soft, blue glow of an iPhone lighting one of our faces. Eventually, I guess, I'll have to abscond with them to the mountains to get their attention. But for now, my boys talk to me, barely pausing to breathe, from the moment their adorable little eyes open to the second they fall asleep, usually in mid-question. I have all the attention I can use.

When my son again mentioned camping the other day, I asked him why he wanted to go. What's so great about camping, after all? He mentioned roasting marshmallows, sleeping outside. But it was much simpler than that, he said, with finality.

"Because it's fun," he answered, looking at me confidently.

Whatever you say, kiddo. We'll see how fun you think it is when you realize there's no WiFi.

(c) 2023 Pioneer Press. All rights reserved. Distributed by Tribune Content Agency, LLC.

Sometimes You Need a Dead Squirrel Disposal Service, and That's OK

June 14, 2021

My husband disposed of a dead body the other day.

I broke the news to him gently.

"Honey, there's an ead-day irrel-squay in the ool-pay," I said, holding the hand of the kid I had just prevented from jumping into the backyard kiddie pool and encountering the grim face of death in the person of one black squirrel, floating, bereft of life, in the water inside.

My husband looked up from his newspaper (yes, an actual newspaper. Like, one made of paper. We're an old-fashioned home).

"Oh *great*," he replied.

For my husband knows that he has always been, and will always be, our family's CDODR, Chief Disposer Of Dead Rodents. He'd previously disposed of several dead mice, but this would be his first foray into squirrels.

For in our home, there is nothing a woman cannot do if she chooses, but there are several things that she chooses not to do, and one of them is touching the waterlogged corpses of tree mammals. Call it the *droit de madame*, the right a woman of the house may exercise, at any time, to avoid tasks she deems sufficiently horrible.

I took our younger son to change his diaper while the real dirty work was being done outside. Getting downstairs afterward, I was surprised to find that my husband was already back on the couch.

"What did you do with it?" I asked.

"Tossed it behind the garage," he said, looking out of the corner of his eye at me.

"What if varmints get to it?"

"Varmints?" he asked with disbelief.

"Yes, varmints," I said. "I think you should throw it in the trash."

He sighed and pulled out his phone.

"What are you doing?" I asked.

"Checking the internet," he said, Googling, I would assume, "what does one do with a dead squirrel?"

I, who have watched a lot of true crime shows like "Dateline," realize that having searches like that in my internet search history could be trouble when the cops show up looking for a squirrel murderer.

And though I do not know how the squirrel actually died, here's what I would have told any investigator who'd asked:

"An elderly squirrel was lying on a tree branch above the pool when he was seized by a massive heart attack! He fell, dead before he hit the water, and wound up, through sheer bad luck and no fault of either of the adults in the house, in the pool."

Eventually, my husband ended his internet searches, sighed deeply and got up.

"Sometimes I regret being born a man," he muttered under his breath as he walked outside to his fate, hands wrapped in a double layer of plastic bags.

Dear reader, I laughed then - a hearty, rolling chuckle, rich with the remembrances of labor pains and hormone injections.

Later, out of the earshot of the kids, I asked him how it had gone.

"Horrible," he said, wrinkling his nose. "I hate doing stuff like that."

He said to get through it, he pictured a drill sergeant, not unlike the one R. Lee Ermey played in "Full Metal Jacket," hollering at him throughout the process.

I felt for him. I really did. I mean, I know sometimes it's hard to be a woman.

There are hills for us to climb, both innate and those created by our culture. We have a tougher time at work, at school and at the doctor's office.

There's pay disparity and unrealistic beauty expectations. Even if we work outside of the home or are the chief breadwinner, we're likely to also be responsible for most of the housework and child care.

We're judged for our personalities and our appearances, whether and how long we breastfeed our children, whether we baby-wear or sleep train, and how early we potty-train our kids.

Heck, we even judge ourselves!

But no matter how hard it gets, ladies, always remember that, if an adult male lives with you and there is a need to dispose of the body of a dead squirrel, you have the right to force that adult male to do it.

Because sometimes it's hard to be a man, too.

(c) 2023 Pioneer Press. All rights reserved. Distributed by Tribune Content Agency, LLC.

In Sickness and in Health, but in 2021, Sickness Won

January 1, 2022

It was two years ago, nearly to the day, that our 5-year-old coined the term "butt puke" to describe diarrhea.

It was an invention of necessity, to explain to us the state in which he had left the bathroom. It painted a vivid picture.

That was the year, 2019, that norovirus and upper respiratory infections ran roughshod through our home, resulting in the memorable Christmas morning when I had to sneak my older son past the festooned and be-presented tree for an emergency room trip, days after we'd visited with the younger one.

It was the year that my father, searching in the middle of the night for a place to, let's just say, burn the candle at both ends, found me curled over the toilet, holding a sick baby on my lap as I vomited inside.

"Oh, no," he said, less from pity than from fear he wouldn't make it to the second bathroom.

Still, though, despite such stiff competition, the Christmas of 2021 will go down in an infamy of infirmity.

My husband was hospitalized multiple times in the weeks running up until the holiday, the third time with a serious blood infection.

"Oh, this could kill you," the ER nurse flippantly replied

after he wondered how dire matters were.

After that, when my mother-in-law asked if she could bring me anything, Xanax came to mind.

Meanwhile, the children and I all came down with the same congested, achy fever that, despite checking every box in the COVID bingo card, provided nothing more than a fusillade of negative tests.

Parents know all too well the COVID test dance. Anytime a kid visits the pediatrician for an upset stomach, cut knee or strange rash, the doctor looks in their eyes, ears and mouth, and then, without fail, orders a COVID test.

Our younger son holds the world's record for Most Consecutive Negative COVID Tests, enough that he now has a preferred kind.

"I hope this isn't the coughing one," he said to me the last time we dragged him to the pediatrician's office to be swabbed.

"It's a bug," the pediatrician announced after his latest negative result.

A bug. It sounded so quaint, like saying he had rickets.

Then, once everything seemed to have settled down, with my invalid husband newly released from the hospital into our feeble embrace, the ceiling started leaking.

Not a flood or anything, just a small, insistent drip, the kind intelligence agencies use to torture spies.

Actually, let me be honest: I did not see the drip. I didn't see it because I was upstairs, bathing the kids, or trying to, before I had to pick the entire operation up and move it to the second bathroom.

My fresh-from-the-hospital husband spent the next day sawing a hole in the ceiling, then calling a plumber who has yet to deign us with his presence.

But no matter.

Because the following day was the day that our toddler, flush with the joy and wonder of the season's first snowfall, crammed his maw so full of snow that he spent the next 24 hours vomiting up whatever dog excrement he'd almost certainly ingested.

We took him to the doctor and they, of course, tested him for COVID.

And that brings me to today.

Multiple hospitalizations, a flurry of doctor visits and more COVID tests than an NBA basketball team and we're left here, with one another, limping into the new year, hoping for a respite and, in some strange way, thankful.

Thankful for the perspective that time brings, the clarity of distance.

Thankful for the sisters and brothers and parents who helped us through.

Thankful that things didn't take the truly foul turn they could have.

I mean, it could be worse.

We do have the second bathroom, after all.

There Are No Monsters Here, Only Those Who Live in Darkness

January 29, 2022

I don't make monster sprays.

Maybe you've seen the pictures of them on Instagram or read about them in parenting blogs: Glittery, colorful placebos, good for chasing away the fearsome creatures in your child's room and mind.

They're harmless enough, I guess, but I've been working hard to provide an alternate storyline for my kids — not that I can magically chase away monsters but that there are none to worry about in the first place.

It's tempting, as a parent, to try to overcome kids' fears (and, frankly, sometimes just get them to go to sleep) by telling them your magic is stronger than monsters.

But lately, I've seen too much of that in our adult world, using boogeymen to control the weak.

Read, for example, an NBC News story about parents consumed with fear that schools use "social emotional learning" to indoctrinate their children with woke propaganda or to introduce ideas of suicide into their young brains.

In that worldview, teachers and school administrators are the evil creatures who want to damage and destroy vulnerable children. They must be literal monsters, after all, to undergo years of education and training in the service of compelling children to suicide and self-hatred.

There's no curriculum that should be immune to dissection and critique. But viewing with such profound distrust the motives of teachers leads to the demonization of an entire profession.

The fearmongering can be, and often is, worse.

Michael Berry, a conservative talk show host who has demanded Nuremberg trials for Democrats, urges his listeners to treat liberals like this:

"Show them no mercy. They showed you none. They are monsters."

But no political party is immune to the lure of the weaponization of fear.

Plenty of so-called progressives attended a recent anti-vaccine rally, for example, where Democrat Robert Kennedy Jr. compared vaccine mandates to the Holocaust.

Those who want everyone to be vaccinated, he said, are monsters — worse, even, than Nazis. At least Anne Frank, he said, got to hide in an attic.

Revolting, but it works.

Fear works. Dehumanization works.

The product — the worldview that monsters want to steal our lives and souls, and those of our children — flies off the shelves. Fear brings power and money.

I mean, we're better in most metrics than ever before. Kids use fewer drugs, have less sex and are more empathetic. We all live longer. Crime is far lower than it was 20 years ago, and charitable giving is up.

But the reality doesn't matter, not when compared to the sexy lure of the horror movie, the jolt of adrenaline we get from being afraid. The jump scare always wins.

Now, I realize that there's plenty to fear. As human as we are, some of us do evil; we are greedy corporate raiders, con artist radio hosts and far, far worse.

But monsters? No. Only those who live in humanity's darkness.

Claiming otherwise distances us, emotionally, from that darkness, but it does so falsely.

It's destructive to believe that we are different, special, better.

It destroys our communities and our relationships, but more critically, it makes us think we're more worthy of good things, that we have earned them with our awesomeness. Instead, we should recognize what an enormous role fortune, good and bad, plays in the paths of our lives.

So maybe we should all stop making monster sprays because there aren't any monsters here, only people.

It does not diminish someone else's crimes to soften our hearts, to remain vigilant against our tendency to exalt ourselves by lowering others.

Empathy is not an excuse. It is a victory.

For in the end, all we need to do to defeat the monsters is turn on the lights. Then, we can see that they were never there in the first place.

Forget Writer's Block; Writer's Remorse Is the Real Pain

February 12, 2022

My husband once asked me if I ever got writer's block.

"No," I answered, with the boundless confidence of fools, "because you know what the cure is? Writing."

And while, technically, yes, I usually do not get writer's block, I do come down with an ailment that's far more debilitating: writer's remorse.

For me, it's easy enough to write.

I can start at the beginning or start at the end. I can jot down a sentence that I like, even if I'm not sure where it will go, and like the frame of a house, build the rest around it.

And inspiration is rarely a problem. I can travel various pathways — stare out the window, use whatever's happening in my life or on social media or in the fevered recesses of my brain.

I've found, however, that the stumbling block often comes later.

There are times — blissful, heady times — when the words flow like water, springing from a well deep inside me, a practically unconscious source. When I read back those words, sometimes I'm confused, marveling at them, not even recognizing myself as their writer.

"Wow," I think, "I wonder who wrote that."

More often, though, I read what I've written and it's like listening to a discordant symphony. I only hear the faulty notes. They clang in my ears, insistent.

That person should seriously consider changing careers.

I can sometimes iron out the wrinkles in a messy first draft, coax the words out of their caves, gently, with treats and soft whispers. I elbow a word over, flip some paragraphs around, work it like a Rubik's cube.

I imagine the intense wave of satisfaction afterward is akin to the feeling a mechanic gets upon fixing the engine in a car.

Listen to that baby purr.

It's rarely so easy.

A former colleague suggested on Twitter that we should put a name to what happens to writers when they can't find the perfect word, le mot juste. Often, we stick in a placeholder but, returning, still can't get the right word. The deadline looms.

We try to talk ourselves into the replacement.

"Maybe that word isn't so bad after all," we say, sweet-talking ourselves. "Maybe that's exactly what I wanted to say in the first place."

That word is *never* what we wanted to say in the first place. It will, each time we read it, for the rest of our lives, give us writer's remorse.

There are times when it's a weak argument or concept that's the problem, when I've gone off half-cocked on something and, upon reflection, realize I was completely full of beans. I've written nonsense.

Though it can be a paralyzing feeling, viewing with fresh eyes your own clownish stupidity, it also can give you empathy when you see it happening to someone else.

"Oh, boy," you think, "that felt wrong immediately, didn't it?"

In fact, plenty of folks could use a little writer's remorse (or speaker's remorse, or tweeter's remorse, as the case may be).

Most of them, though, just give birth to their asinine thoughts and abandon them in the woods to be raised by wolves, never considering that they might need a little tending to mature into a grown-up, functional opinion.

I suppose, when it comes to writer's block, or even writer's remorse, it's not always a bad thing.

Stopping, thinking, revising and revisiting, they all can be tools and they all can serve a purpose.

Maybe, though, the next time someone asks me about writer's block, I won't get so cocky, if for no other reason than things can always get worse.

A Parent's Least-Favorite Sci-Fi Movie: 'Invasion of the Bed-Snatchers'

March 5, 2022

They come at night.

We're unconscious, as insensible to our surroundings as if we'd been slipped a stupefying drug or deprived of quality sleep for the past six years.

They enter our bedroom, the aliens do, sometimes silently, sometimes throwing the door open and jumping into the bed as if escaping the path of an oncoming train.

"Mom!" they might yell. "I had a scary dream!"

Other times they're cold or thirsty or have a cough.

We motion them into bed, pull the covers up and listen to their hastily recounted nightmares — the guy with no face, the clown on wheels, the witch — and try to get them back to sleep.

Invariably groggy, we fail to recognize that *this* is the key moment, the time when we will decide whether to trudge across the cold floor and lose a little sleep getting them back into their own beds or give up the fight in service of warm feet and staying horizontal.

There are two in the conversation: Nighttime Parent and Daytime Parent.

"Come on," Daytime Parent says to Nighttime Parent. "Just take them back to their own bed and sit there with them for a couple of minutes while they fall back asleep."

Nighttime Parent's response:

"Go pound sand."

And so, we sleep — or try to, more accurately. One of the kids quickly works himself perfectly horizontal, pushing against the nearest back with his feet as forcefully as if he were trying to launch himself into space. Parents cling to the bed's cliff, holding on to a wafer-thin scrap of mattress.

Then, in comes the second bed-snatcher to complete the invasion. You're powerless, frozen in their tractor beams.

You can't very well reject one kid when the other is snoozing blissfully between his parents like a prudish dance chaperone who won't let the couple get too close.

Before you know it, there are four in the bed.

Someone always has an unfair amount of acreage and it's never an adult.

It's possible, sometimes, to relocate one or both bed-snatchers back to their own room, but it must be done carefully, quietly, with the same delicacy one reserves for defusing a bomb.

First, you must inch your arms under the shoulders and knees of the child, bending over in a way that is certain to remind you in the morning of your advancing age and imminent death.

Then, you stand, your knees straightening with a horrible creak. This might wake one or both of the bed-snatchers, leading to wailing and forcing a complete reset of the process.

Even if it works, when you get to their room, you must maneuver them into a freezing-cold bed and pull up freezing-cold covers over a body that had, until just moments earlier, been warmed by a parental comforter.

Should you defy the odds and succeed, now you have to do it all over again with the other one.

This is, also, no guarantee that they'll stay put. Just as often, they'll re-colonize your bed the second you fall back asleep, and there's no way you're moving them twice in one night.

Take us to your leader, one of the aliens might say.

The only problem is, *they're* the leaders — at least when

you're too tired to fight.

It's a shame, really, but the sooner you come to terms with your fate, the easier your life will be.

Accept it. Don't struggle.

As the Borg say, resistance is futile.

In any case, one day, the bed-snatching will end. You'll have your space to yourself, then, every night, forever and always.

And that's when you'll really have something to cry about.

A Colonoscopy To Remember, and a Prep To Forget

March 19, 2022

I recently had a colonoscopy and let me tell you, it was wonderful.

I say that because getting the colonoscopy meant the colonoscopy prep was over. And starting the colonoscopy prep meant I could stop dreading the whole process.

You see, the only thing worse than a colonoscopy is preparing for a colonoscopy; and the only thing worse than *that* is the anticipation.

Well, no, that's wrong. Learning I have cancer that could have been caught earlier if I'd only subjected myself to a day of discomfort would be worse.

And that's why I decided to do it.

"It" being drinking four liters of osmotic laxatives, then rushing to the bathroom so many times that my 5-year-old started to exclaim, "The potty? *Again?*" each time I was mid-sprint.

The laxatives prepared my bowels for the procedure, during which, apparently, they needed to be as clear as the rushing water in a cold mountain spring.

Drinking from the jug and pondering what it was doing to my insides, I was reminded of watching my Greek grandmother make magiritsa, a traditional Easter dish, so many years ago.

"What's that?" I asked my dad as my grandmother held one end of a hazy white tube to the faucet.

"Lamb intestines," he responded. When he saw the look on my face, he gave a dismissive wave. "Don't worry, she cleans them really well."

I guess if my grandmother could make intestines clean enough to eat, these industrial-strength laxatives could make mine clean enough to stick a camera into.

As I drank, I read the papers the pharmacy had included with the "prep" liquid, which I was informed would be lemon-lime flavored.

Lemon-lime, indeed.

It actually tasted more like a vat of lukewarm spittle over which a particularly malevolent leprechaun had half-heartedly waved a moldy lemon.

"We can get civilians into space, but we can't make something that tastes better than this?" I complained to my sister-in-law.

One feels food scientists should redirect their efforts, at least temporarily, from making mac and cheese that tastes like Cheetos to improving the flavor of these laxatives.

The pharmacy's instructions said sucking on a lemon drop might make the drink more palatable, but I can't drink 3 liters of anything — not chocolate milk, not freshly squeezed orange juice, not ice-cold sauvignon blanc.

The best part of the prep was that my stomach was too full of what my husband called "joy juice" to complain about the fact that I hadn't had any solid food for 24 hours.

When my kids asked why I had to keep drinking, I stammered.

"Well ... the doctor needs my insides cleared out ... so they can put a camera ..."

"Up her butt," my husband finished, helpfully.

The boys gave me shocked looks.

"Is it going to hurt?" one asked.

"Absolutely not," I replied. "I won't even feel it."

And not only was that true, but I wasn't afraid, either. I wasn't even awake.

The last thing I remembered on C-Day was the doctor telling me I might taste something a little "spicy." I tried to stay awake, curious about the procedure, but couldn't.

The next thing I knew, I was trying to get up.

"I have to use the bathroom," I said, when the nurse moved me back down to a lying position.

"No, you don't," she replied. "You just had a colonoscopy."

Well, what does that have to do with anything? I wondered.

Eventually, I remembered I couldn't possibly have to use the bathroom. There was nothing in my intestines to expel.

As it turned out, there was no cancer in there, either.

I'm relieved, not just from seeing the end of the procedure but from the hope that by the time another one rolls around, maybe scientists will have discovered all the potential Oreo cookie flavors and will move on to improving the prep liquid.

Sauvignon blanc flavor, anyone?

When There's Nothing You Can Do, Build a Fire

April 9, 2022

I like to build fires.

When it's chilly but not bitter, overcast but not raining, there's nothing more satisfying than dragging out our rusty, hand-me-down fire pit and making a blaze.

I gather armfuls of twigs, grab a couple of large logs from the garage and twist up some newspaper. I use an old blue lighter that I keep on the back porch for just such occasions, and after I start the fire up, I like to toss in another handful of newspaper or leaves to get it really roaring.

From time to time, I use a wide stick I've saved to remove the fire pit's cage, then stir the ashes or poke the burning logs.

I might sit nearby, pulling the tape off a cardboard box, tearing it into strips and feed those in, too.

I watch the fire, move my chair out of the smoke if the wind direction changes and think about nothing, everything.

My kids have dispersed long ago, bored of collecting sticks from the yard, but I can still see them inside, through the windows. They watch TV or play in the living room, and occasionally, I scroll aimlessly through my phone, but more often, I put it in my pocket and leave it there.

I start to smell the smoke on my clothes, in my hair, and

it smells like my childhood, like bonfires on the beach and a taverna's souvlaki grill.

It's the same fire my ancestors have sat in front of for hundreds, thousands, millions of years.

It's reality and yet it's relaxing. It feels like doing something but isn't.

"What are you doing back there?" my husband might ask if I've been outside for a particularly long time.

"Nothing," I answer, the truth. "Just building a fire."

I hate camping, but I love fires. Camping is work, and once you're out there, you're stuck. You can't just get up and walk inside when you get too cold or make a cup of hot tea in your own kitchen just because you had a hankering for it.

But with a fire, I'm still there, sort of, in nature, and there are trees and grass and there's the slight discomfort of "outdoors" in the cold weather.

Like a meditation, it's immediate.

More and more these days, I try to find that "now," remind myself that places like Instagram and Netflix and Twitter aren't my life.

Because those places can touch me — maybe I've seen a show or read a story that makes me angry or jealous or sad — but they touch me from somewhere else, move me from outside and reveal events happening in another place or time.

No matter how important, no matter how real, they're not right now, right here, where I am.

And that's all I'm guaranteed: right now.

I may be able to take action, create art, show my love, but if I don't find joy in the now, I am missing my life's true purpose.

Everything changes.

We grow old; we die. Our friends can drift away, and our family can disappear and change.

We're under constant threat from life's ugliness, from the coldness. There's war. There's suffering. There's hatred and pettiness and mean-spirited politics.

And no matter what we do with our lives, we can never

eliminate that ugliness entirely. The coldness will come, every year.

But it's not always bad, is it, to be caught in the cold?

Because when it seems like the outdoors are barren and cruel, when I'm shivering my way through the long, harsh spring that stretches out for miles, there's something I can do.

I can always build a fire.

Childhood Performance More of a Focus Than Ever Before

May 7, 2022

Our children are anxious, and they're getting more so every day.

Even before the pandemic, anxiety among the kids in our country was increasing at an alarming rate, and the situation has only gotten worse.

I'm not a psychologist or a researcher, but I am a parent, and it's incumbent upon me to give my kids the best chance at mental health.

Some factors parents cannot choose: the genes we've passed along to our children that make them more susceptible to anxiety, the unavoidable tough patches in life, and the friends they'll make, friends who will either reinforce or contradict their parents' approach.

We can choose, however, the amount of pressure we put on children to achieve.

I've been thinking about that a lot lately, as our kids' schools have begun to emphasize scholastic performance at earlier and earlier ages.

Recently, my husband and I attended a parent-teacher conference for our 3-year-old (an activity in which I feel certain my own parents would not have had either the opportunity or the desire to engage). At the meeting, one of our son's teachers mentioned that he wasn't up to speed on some of his shapes.

"Buy flashcards," she suggested.

Her comment concerned me, not because I had any intention of quizzing my toddler on what a rhombus is, but because I'm sure there are other parents who, worried their child might be falling behind his fellow preschoolers, would.

In fact, one classmate was recently moved to another room after his mom said he wasn't "learning anything."

Gosh, not having to learn anything is the best part about preschool, I thought when the boy's nanny explained why he was in a different classroom now.

Our older child is in kindergarten, and when report cards were sent home, I didn't even read the academic portion. Frankly, I don't care whether he's testing at grade level.

What I want to know is this:

Is he kind?

Is he learning to behave, to make friends, to put on his coat and rainboots without help?

A few weeks later, the kindergarten teacher sent home an activity for the kids, a plastic baggie filled with cut-out words from a list they're supposed to know.

We were told to pull the words out one by one, to quiz them to see which they could read. She also suggested making a wall chart and pointing at words every time the kids go past.

The goal is for them to be able to read 50 words by the end of the year.

I promptly put the bag of words away and soon lost them, something I only feel a little bad about. The guilt isn't because I think I'm falling behind on instructing my child but because I know the teacher went through a not-insignificant amount of trouble to put together the activity.

The care she took in creating the assignment leads me to believe she, or someone else at the school, thinks there's value to drilling, rote memorization and achievement, even at this early stage.

I can't help but think, though, of my memories of kindergarten, of snacks and naptimes, games and coloring sheets. I don't recall a test or a subject, or even a single thing that I "learned."

My sons will have exactly one shot at the magical time of early childhood, and I refuse to have it sullied with successes and failures. I don't feel any anxiety about their performance, and I hope they don't, either.

And if they ever ask how they did, I will simply tell them God's honest truth:

"Honey, you got straight As."

Back to School, Back to the Everyday Miseries of Childhood

September 3, 2022

The kids are back to school.

I know that because today, for the first time in three months, I worked out.

Yes, I know that I could and should work out even when the kids are home. But I also shouldn't be eating leftover mac and cheese and cold chicken nuggets for dinner and, sorry to say, that just happens sometimes. In parenting, exhaustion often defeats willpower.

It's true that, as a parent, you need balance. On one side of the scale are your children's needs, and those are paramount. They weigh more than your needs, which often (but hopefully not always) come second.

Now that the kids are in school again, I have the chance to even the scales a bit. I can add more to my side — write, work out, maybe grocery shop without saying "put that down" 1,000 times in a row.

I've also mostly recovered from the horrors of the school supply list, which gets longer and weirder every year. This year, I had to purchase beans (yes, *beans*), not one but two cans of shaving cream and boxes of pasta. I don't know how many macaroni necklaces one kid can make, but I did as I was told.

Both of our kids were less than thrilled to return to the classroom. The first grader resentfully trundled out of the car every day for a week before his younger brother went back to school.

"Why does he get more summer than I do?" the 6-year-old asked.

"The older you get, the harder life is," I told him, and though in some ways that's true, it occurred to me later that it's not entirely so.

The realization came as I was serving as a "lunch helper" at the elementary school, a task mostly consisting of withstanding the aural battering of 100 first graders eating lunch in the same room.

As I opened innumerable milk cartons and potato-chip bags, I looked around at the kids and saw that the social strata were already in place.

Some children nervously walked the room holding trays of food, looking for a spot near a friend or friendly face. Others were the Masters of the Universe, holding court in groups of acolytes.

There was the ease of childhood on display but there was also anxiety and fear, fear of danger as imminent as any adult faces in their daily life.

As lunchtime concluded, one of the teachers told the kids to pack up and go outside for recess. The students scrambled up and out of the cafeteria. The last to leave was a skinny boy wearing glasses. He sat quietly, tears streaming down his face, as he hurriedly stuffed food in his mouth.

He didn't look like a Master of the Universe. More likely, he was one of those who'd had trouble finding a spot. None of the other kids had waited for him.

A teacher came up to him and offered a napkin, ostensibly to wipe his hands.

She sat and talked with him quietly for a minute, and once he was done eating, he wiped his face with his hands and walked outside.

It broke my heart, and it reminded me how difficult childhood can be — not even in any large, terrible way but just in the everyday ways, the ways that include not finding someone to sit next to at lunchtime.

They're the ways that slumber parties and cafeterias and playgrounds can be harsh. And it's not that you forget those experiences when you age, but you can forget how small they might appear to someone on the outside, to an adult.

After that day in the lunchroom, I told myself that I'll try to be more sensitive to the little agonies my children face, the daily miseries that aren't bigger or smaller than those in my life, at least when they're shown to scale.

Their worlds are smaller, after all, and so are the stressors and sadness.

Seen from a child's perspective, however, they're exactly the same size.

Fake Eyelashes, First-Grade Math and Other Problems

November 12, 2022

I learned this week that first-grade math is too hard, my joints are falling apart and fake eyelashes are a demonic creation.

First, my son came home with a word problem. We sat down at the kitchen table to read:

"If there are twice as many blue balloons as red balloons and two more yellow balloons than green balloons, why is Elon Musk spending so much time arguing with Stephen King on Twitter?"

"Isn't this ... *algebra?*" I grumbled while scribbling furiously on a sheet of scratch paper.

"What's algebra?" my son asked.

"It's really hard math," I said as the sweat popped up on my forehead. "Math that Mommy didn't do so hot at in school, which is why she ended up a journalist."

"Three yellow balloons!" my 4-year-old exclaimed in delight.

Eventually, between the three of us, we solved the problem, but then I decided to put on fake eyelashes.

At the drug store, I also bought fake nails, the super-long kind that make it impossible to type, open a soda can or wipe your butt.

Maybe I thought the lashes and nails would make me look more feminine. I've cut off most of my hair, to help grow out the gray quicker, and from certain angles I look a little too much like my brother.

So, one fine day, while the kids were at school, I devoted myself to applying the lashes.

I took them out of their packaging and held one up, close to my face so I could see without my glasses.

I uncapped the glue and squeezed. Black liquid bubbled out all over my hand.

"No sweat," I said cheerfully, heading to the sink.

Second try: Hold the lashes, squint and dab a little glue ...

There! Now, wait for it to dry.

And wait. And wait.

OK, that should be fine. Near the lash line but not too close — Well. Hm.

Now I had two rows of eyelashes, one about a half-inch higher than the other.

Didn't Elizabeth Taylor have two rows of eyelashes?

I decided to figure it out later and focus on the other side.

More glue this time, I thought as I squeezed a hefty glob onto the fake lashes. Glue ran down all over my fingers.

I'll clean that up later.

After waiting for the glue to dry, I applied the lashes. The instant I touched them to my face, black glue flowed out over my eyelid and into my eye, which instantly began to burn.

I comforted myself with the thought that if the glue blinded me, I could retire after the lawsuit.

I ran back to the sink. Pulling at the eyelashes, one row flipped off and almost went down the drain.

I should let it go, I thought.

My hands and face were black. The congealing glue had turned into tiny, bug-like dots, and my eyes were surrounded by black slime.

"Looking good," the mirror said.

I realized then that I was going to be late for physical

therapy, which I'm getting for "moderate osteoarthritis" that my doctor charitably told me I'm a "little young for."

The physical therapist threatened me with a hip replacement so I can't miss even a single appointment.

In retrospect, probably not the best time to put on fake eyelashes.

I scrubbed furiously with my fingers and toilet paper and, in a particularly ill-advised move, hand soap, until it finally all came off. It only took 20 minutes and my last scrap of dignity.

Thankfully, the glue, the math problem and the physical therapy appointment are all in the past now.

I'm left only with the memories and the priceless knowledge that my eyelashes are fine as they are.

Maybe I'll wait until next week to put on the fake nails.

Is 'M3GAN' Babysitter-Worthy?

January 28, 2023

You're a parent. You're busy. And, if you're anything like me, the last time you paid to see a movie in the theater, it was back when we thought COVID would be over by the time Pete Davidson had found another out-of-his-league woman to date.

But maybe you're ready to get out there again. Maybe you saw "Top Gun: Maverick" in the theater and thought: "Hey, I remember this! Popcorn! Candy! Watching a movie without falling asleep on the couch halfway through!"

With that in mind, I watched the new movie "M3GAN" with the intent of reviewing it for the great uncool masses — for parents.

Running time: 1 hour, 42 minutes. My husband wanted to see "Avatar: The Way of the Water," which has a 3-hour, 12-minute running time. Show me a 3-hour-long movie and I'll show you a director who hasn't seen the inside of a grocery store in at least 20 years. There's something particularly obnoxious about a science fiction director who thinks it's better that his audience gets UTIs than he cut an hour out of his movie. It's not "Schindler's List." It's about blue people. I haven't seen it and I can already tell you what to cut: The part where the camera slowly pans around the computer-generated seascape for 20 minutes. While my husband was stuck in "Avatar: Which Way to the Restroom?" for so long that his clothes went out of style, I watched a movie, then ambled around the mall window-shopping. I picked out two handmade Ukrainian Christmas ornaments in an after-season sale. I bought and ate a warm pretzel covered in butter and salt. My husband said everyone watching "Avatar" missed at least one key scene while they were going to the bathroom. I only gloated a little bit afterward.

Cast: The main character is played by that one woman from that one show where they were trying to shock you all the time with the nudity and sex and drug use. You know, the show I tried to watch but stopped after finally admitting to myself I'm not as carefree and cool as I would like to be. She's the actress whose dad is famous, too. He was a news anchor and then there was a scandal. I think he said he stormed the beaches of Normandy and then it came out he was just at home eating ice cream and watching Netflix? Anyway, her. And then there's a guy in "M3GAN"; he's from "Crazy Rich Asians" but not the hot guy. I mean, he's OK, just he's no Henry Golding is all. He's funny, though.

Plot: "M3GAN" is "Chucky" on TikTok. It's scary but not too scary, silly but not dumb and fun but not obnoxious. It also had something going for it that very few movies do these days: It featured a staggering lack of politics. "M3GAN" wasn't about global warming or race relations or the collective trauma we've suffered as a result of the green M&M having her high heels taken away. One of the best things about movies is the way they allow us to turn our brains off for the short time we're watching (or for the really, really long time, if it's a James Cameron movie). Oscar-bait movies notwithstanding, the best films are the ones that entertain as much as, if not more than, they challenge. I've never been a fan of movies that seem to think that the more the audience suffers, the more artistically worthwhile the film is. Morals are fine, sure, but only when painted with a light touch. The only moral to be learned from "M3GAN" is that parents who give their kids too much screen time are basically turning them into serial killers. *Yawn.* Moms already feel horrible, crippling guilt every time they turn on an electronic device for their kids. Do your worst, Hollywood.

The upshot: When it comes to the ultimate test, whether or not "M3GAN" is babysitter-worthy, I say yes. And you won't fall asleep in the middle of it. Unless you have a newborn, in which case, may I suggest "Avatar"?

Child-Free Adults Aren't Lazy — Parenting Has Gotten Harder

February 11, 2023

We've just taken down the Christmas decorations, snow's falling outside my window and a fireplace roars before me.

In other words, it's time to start worrying about summer camp.

There are options — oh, are there options — and if I'm not online at 10 a.m. sharp when registration opens, my kids might be stuck going to a summer camp for those with an interest in tax accounting.

I pore over brochures, scribbling down dates, texting to see where other kids are going. I plan summer six months in advance. My hair's starting to fall out, but the good news is that it's so gray it's harder to tell.

And that, my friends, is the reason for the global declining birthrate.

It's fashionable these days to accuse young people of being lazy or selfish for not wanting to trade their child-free independence for parental servitude.

But the opposite is true. It's not that young people have gotten softer, it's that parenting has gotten harder.

In past generations, good parenting consisted of providing three healthy meals a day and a bed to sleep in. For most of human history, occasional hugs and kisses were considered borderline spoiling.

Now, though, parents must maximize their children's social, psychological, spiritual, physical and emotional development. From the moment kids eat their home-cooked, low-sugar, vegan breakfasts to the second they fall asleep in their organic, VOC-free, non-fire-retardant mattresses, children must be comforted, supported, validated and challenged in every way.

The results of failure are anxiety, depression, obesity, ill health and lifelong unemployment — so, no pressure.

Being a perfect parent has never been possible, but only recently have we been constantly bombarded with images of people who are doing it better. If you manage not to beat yourself for making a mistake, parents on Instagram/Facebook/TikTok are happy to do it for you.

"Oh, I see you got your kids Happy Meals for dinner. I wish I didn't care about my little Braxton's health so much that I could feed him poison without feeling guilty. If you ever decide you might want to cook something healthy, I have a great recipe for baked seaweed and pumpkinseed fries."

Usually, though, we don't need anyone to criticize us. We do a perfectly fine job on our own.

I saw a mom comment the other day about how she felt guilty for letting her 2-year-old watch too much TV while she and her husband were both sick. (I should add that the mom was, in addition to being sick, also pregnant.)

How horrifying for a woman of childbearing age to read that, to know that if she decides to procreate, that's the kind of life she's in for: guilt, self-castigation and always feeling that you're falling short.

We tell our children that outcomes don't matter, that it's about putting in the effort and doing your best, but they see us treating ourselves differently. Being a good parent isn't about trying to be a good parent but about punishing yourself when you fail to reach perfection.

I've never believed much in shame, as a strategy. It doesn't stop behaviors, only makes someone feel bad about them.

It's the same for parenting. We need breaks, and kids like TV and delicious food. To shame us (or them) for that just results in parental guilt (and a kid who thinks anything short of ideal is intolerable).

And after all this, I'll still register them for summer camp. But once it's done, it's done. No sense in second-guessing or feeling guilty about the decisions.

Camp should be fun, shouldn't it? For kids, at least. And for parents, well, at least they're not watching TV. (Not that there's anything wrong with that!)

Moms, Don't Get Stuck in the Gratitude Trap

March 4, 2023

Let me be clear: I enjoy being a parent.

I enjoy hugging my kids. I enjoy tucking them in at night. I enjoy when they eat something I've made and exclaim, "Mommy, this is so good!" I enjoy how their brains work. I enjoy watching them learn new things, gaining confidence. I enjoy the hilarious, silly and sweet things they say.

But I don't enjoy everything, and I don't enjoy it all the time.

I don't enjoy it when one of them is sick or hurt. I don't enjoy how they sneak into our bed every night, splaying themselves out like sheiks in repose. I don't enjoy the state in which they leave the bathroom.

In the grand tradeoff, the "loves" easily outweigh the "don't loves," and I'll never say otherwise.

But despite that, I don't appreciate the guilt. Not guilt thrust upon me by my progeny, no. Guilt handed me by fellow parents — mothers, if I'm honest — for looking with dread upon any part of parenting, no matter how loathsome.

I encountered that maternal guilt trip, again, recently, in the form of a mommy blog post about how important it is for mothers to constantly remind themselves to feel joy and gratitude for their status as a parent.

"I am living the halcyon years," the writer said of her children's messes, tantrums and screaming, the tough but unavoidable days (or weeks or years) that few parents tolerate with anything approaching grace.

She admitted in the post to being "guilty" of not enjoying those moments, of not being properly grateful.

How dare she, I asked myself sarcastically. How dare she not pause, covered in baby barf and woozy from two hours of sleep, and remind herself that any feeling short of pure ecstasy is a betrayal?

These are the same assurances mothers have always been given: "One day, you'll miss it."

I, for one, call BS.

My kids are firmly out of the baby stage, and though I do sometimes spend an hour scrolling through photos of them in adorable onesies, and though I do sometimes feel nostalgic, I also eventually remember how glad I am that my parental work in the baby mines is completed.

I remember the terrible reflux that caused one baby to spit up so much and so often I stopped changing my clothes every time. I remember the day I fully understood why sleep deprivation is used as torture. I remember changing dirty diapers in airplane bathrooms and the trunks of cars and on my lap in a restaurant toilet.

Those times? I don't miss them much.

I am happy that my children now use the bathroom and eat solid food and sleep for 10 hours straight, and I don't feel guilty for that. Nor should I.

There is such pressure on mothers, such an impossible standard, and I refuse to add to that weight the additional burden of gratitude, perfect and ever-present.

It's not my children's fault that I have to drive them everywhere and cook their every meal and wash their every piece of clothing, but it's not my fault that I don't always like it, either. And I don't feel bad about occasionally looking forward to not doing those things, the same way I once looked forward to my kids being able to walk, talk and wipe their own butts.

So, if, like me, you are one of those imperfect mothers — sometimes ungrateful, sometimes bored, sometimes tired —-take heart.

You're doing the work. You're loving your children. You're caring for their every need. You're raising them up.

And I say — and here you are free to accept or reject my advice — well, I say that's enough.

You don't have to always enjoy it, too.

Mediocre People Need Influencers, Too

March 25, 2023

I wish there were influencers for the rest of us: We the imperfect. We the mediocre. We the normal.

That's what occurred to me lately as I watched famed influencer/actress/dieter Gwyneth Paltrow discuss what she eats (or, more accurately, doesn't eat) in a typical day.

In the video, she said she fasts until noon. Before then, she drinks something like coffee — nothing that raises her blood sugar. For lunch, she has "bone broth," and for dinner, "lots of cooked vegetables."

She relayed all this while wearing an IV that she said had vitamins in it.

I'm not surprised she needs a vitamin IV if her daily caloric intake is mostly composed of what they give to hospitalized people incapable of digesting solid food.

If anyone's interested in my daily diet, I'm happy to share.

After dropping the kids off at school, I eat a few bites of cold scrambled eggs, bananas and waffles as I'm throwing away the rest of their perfectly good food.

Come lunchtime, I root through the fridge for leftovers. Maybe I'll make an omelet out of chicken tenders and fries, mixed with diced tomatoes and onions from leftover gyros toppings.

Failing that, what has an approaching expiration date? Is there something the kids brought home, untouched, from the previous day's lunch?

For dinner, I'll have lemon-baked cod drizzled lightly with olive oil, steamed broccoli and brown basmati rice, and drink sparkling water over ice. Either that or a chopped salad of ditalini pasta, bacon and blue cheese (possibly also containing lettuce, though I wouldn't swear to it), covered in creamy Italian dressing, followed by deep-dish pepperoni pizza, red wine and brownies.

It's not aspirational, sure. But mediocrity can sometimes be better.

An illustration: After dropping my son off at preschool the other day, I sat in my car, fiddling with the radio. Suddenly, a woman whipped open my driver's side front door, obviously thinking it was her car.

She clutched her chest and gasped as if I'd jumped out of the bushes wearing only a trench coat and a grin.

I looked at her in confusion, but before I could process what happened, she'd shut the door and walked away. Nary an apology or explanation to be had.

Maybe she was offended that I had the nerve to drive around in a car that looked so much like hers.

Really, though, it didn't. As she pulled out of the spot next to me, I saw her car and yes, while one black SUV looks a lot like another black SUV, my car cost about $40,000 less and is covered in a light patina of road salt and dirt. I think it adds to the intrigue.

"Why's her car so dirty?" people probably wonder. "Has she been to the mountains recently? Does she do a lot of off-roading?"

Also, one of my headlights is broken and the body shop won't do the repairs until after the insurance approves the charges and I can't wash the car until the light gets fixed and ... well, you don't need the backstory. What's important is, her car didn't look that much like mine. Maybe I should have jumped out of my car and hopped into hers, I thought later. Traded up.

But it's so much pressure to drive around in a pristine car.

What if someone bumps into you at the grocery store? What if your kids insist on rubbing their muddy boots on every interior surface each time they climb into their seats? Isn't it exhausting to have nice things?

And Gwyneth's diet's gotta be exhausting, too. Just changing out the vitamin IVs must be a tremendous hassle. For an influencer, she's doing a poor job of influencing me to want her lifestyle.

Instead, maybe I'll keep looking for my influencer, the person who posts Instagram photos and TikTok videos showing mediocrity's glamorous side. She'll revel in the joys of being average and sell me on the imperfect lifestyle.

It won't take too much influencing, honestly.

I must say, I'm already sold.

A Trip to the Aquarium — Borderline Educational, Seriously Expensive

April 1, 2023

It's spring break and the kids are home from school, so I recently decided to drop the equivalent of a decent-sized car payment on a trip to the aquarium.

I'd signed them up for a camp for a couple of hours a day, but after that was canceled, we were left with only screen-based diversions.

"Why does it keep saying 'We'll be right back'?" my older son asked about the cartoons he'd been watching, cartoons from the olden days.

"It used to have a commercial there," I explained.

"Ugh," he said, rolling his eyes. "Why can't they just cut that out?"

That's when I decided to take them to the aquarium.

The next day, we piled into the car.

"I'm bored," one kid said during the drive.

"I was bored all the time when I was a kid," I responded.

Boredom, in fact, was the chief feature of my childhood. I was bored when it rained, bored in cars and on planes and standing in line with my mom at the grocery store.

Even when the TV was on, I was usually bored. I didn't want to watch the news or football or "Matlock." I wanted to watch cartoons, and those were only on for about an hour and a half after school and then for a luxurious four hours on Saturday.

But like all children before them, my kids don't want to hear my complaints. They feel a little sorry for me, but mostly my sob stories just bore them.

At the aquarium, I paid an extortionate sum for parking, then walked for 20 minutes from the lot to the aquarium's front door. Once inside, I requested two children's and one adult ticket.

$127?

I briefly considered instead taking them to a restaurant with a lobster tank. We'd even have something to eat afterward.

Eventually, though, I acquiesced, paid and we were inside, where we were treated to a panoply of sea creatures — everything from jellyfish to sea otters. My kids were definitely almost partially entertained.

They were, however, enraptured with one part: Inside a glass case, an aquarium employee rearranged the plants inside the Amazon rainforest exhibit.

"He's standing in the water!" my kids exclaimed. I had to drag them away, reassuring them that they could watch people care for plants at home, promising that I'd let them know the next time I was about to prune the rosebush.

Soon, we entered another spot that impressed them mightily: the gift shop.

I'd had enough of fighting the costs and rolled over like my snoring husband after a prodding.

"Can I have this stuffed dolphin?" one child asked.

"Yes."

"Me, too?"

"The same one?"

He nodded.

"Fine."

I even paid for the $5 plastic bag they sell so they don't have to hand out plastic bags. That's fine with me, just as it was fine with me that the aquarium cafeteria didn't have plastic straws. You know, to save the environment. They were thoughtful enough to give you a giant plastic cup when you ask for a straw.

"Good thing you're not giving out straws!" I thought as I put the cups on the tray.

After lunch, and more wandering, we left the aquarium. My older son dragged his feet, worn out from the day.

"Come on," I said, "pick up the pace."

I feel like I'm always ordering them around.

Do this, don't do that. Hurry up, don't run. Stop touching that, here hold this. I must sound like an impossible scold. Without my drill sergeant instructions, though, everything goes to pot.

As we walked the mile or so back to the parking lot, my son asked me a question.

"You know what I'm tired of?"

"No. What?"

"Walking," he said, and that's when I knew for sure that he was my child.

"Me, too," I said, finally loading us, our stuffed dolphins and plastic bags into the car at the end of the day — exhausted, a little bit educated and seriously financially depleted.

But on the plus side, at least it'll give them something to complain about when they get older.

Crying Babies Stink, but So Do Adults Who Freak Out About Them

April 22, 2023

Did you see the video of the guy freaking out because of a crying baby on a plane?

I did, and I'll be reliving images from it in my nightmares for years to come.

The man completely lost it on the flight attendants, his co-passengers and anyone else within shouting distance. He screamed and cursed, insisting that the parents shut their kid up, and refused to be calmed. After an airline employee admonished him, saying he was yelling, he screamed in response:

"So is the baby!"

It wasn't so much his reaction to the crying — as over-the-top as it was — as much as it was imagining being that baby's parents.

There's no way they (or anyone else on the plane) could have avoided hearing the diatribe, and I'm certain that there existed a crescendo of grousing on the man's part indicating his increased annoyance with the baby, and them. If there was anything they could have done to stop their child's crying, they would have done it.

Snacks, videos, walks, toys — whatever weapons the kid's parents had, they deployed them.

Eventually, though, they were left there, with a baby who couldn't be pacified and an adult who couldn't be cool about it.

We've all been there.

Our kids have been inconvenient, unreasonable and frustrating, often to us but occasionally to people who did not choose to bring them into the world, and it never feels good.

But the negative reactions seem to have gotten worse lately. In the comments on the video, I saw parents called "breeders" and children called "crotch fruit," nasty characterizations of the adults as selfish and their progeny as entitled monsters.

A shocking number of people seem to have forgotten that they, also, were once children, and that plenty of others were forced to suffer their irritating-but-developmentally-appropriate behaviors. They claim to have had parents who wrestled them into submission at the merest whiff of brattiness or claim to be parents who always adeptly finagled perfect compliance from their kids.

I'm not so sure.

They may think they or their parents were the model of military discipline, but every parent has had moments where they were too tired, distracted or powerless to control every variable. They couldn't stop every tantrum or prepare themselves for every eventuality.

I guarantee that they or their children were also, at times, annoying.

But really, I think, this is a little bit about COVID.

Now, hear me out.

For years, we've been getting gradually less accustomed to inconvenience. We've spent the great majority of three years being in our homes, surrounded in relative comfort, spending time almost exclusively with those to whom we are related or tied in emotional bonds.

Many of us didn't even, for months, have the most basic interactions. At the height of the pandemic, my kids played a game they called "Groceries" where one would fill a shopping bag with items and then yell "Instacart!" before running away.

We're all a little rusty when it comes to dealing with the unexpected and the uncomfortable. We're less patient with crying babies on airplanes, bad drivers on the highway — really, anyone who confronts us with the tiresome reality that we're not alone in the world.

That, considering what we've been through, is natural.

But so are crying babies.

And I hope that as time passes, and we're pushed into close quarters with each other more and more often, that hair trigger will relax a little.

We'll see that inside all the annoying other people on earth are just folks like us — folks who just want to take their kid to see grandma for Easter and who don't want to listen to their baby cry any more than you do.

Then we'll pop on a pair of earbuds, order a stiff drink and relax into the bothersome but magical truth that we're all simply human beings.

Heck, the next time it's my kid who's annoying, I'm buying.

Technology Tricks Us, but We Are Our Own Best Gadgets

April 29, 2023

I recently forgot that I have a neck.

It happened as I backed out of a grocery store parking space. I noticed my car's rearview camera lens was so dirty that I could no longer see through it.

I started to panic, worried I was going to hit someone.

But I was already halfway out of the spot! It was hopeless! What could I do?

"Wait," I suddenly realized. "I can just ... turn my head and look behind me."

It turns out that, all along, my head has been equipped with its very own rearview camera.

But that's how technology works. We think it makes our lives easier, but it actually makes them harder, only in a different way.

Case in point: car seats.

When I was a kid, car seats were for babies, and babies only.

Once you were old enough to hold your head up, you had a regular seat, with a lap belt — unless it was a long car ride, in which case you curled up in a ball on the floor, or you were in a pickup, in which case you and seven other kids sat in the truck bed, rattling around like candy in a pinata.

There have been innumerable safety improvements since those days, and now parents are advised to keep their kids in car seats until they turn 25 years old or move out of the house, whichever comes first.

Car seats keep kids safer — if you can figure out how to install them.

I had to remove both of our car seats recently, to put them into a rental car, and believe me when I say that whatever technological improvements have been made to car seat safety have not extended to their installation.

I began the series of 400 steps required to unhook the seats — pressing buttons, unclipping straps and moving levers. Eventually, though, I could go no further. One strap was stuck, closed tighter than Rupert Murdoch's fist around a $20 bill. No matter how hard I pulled, it wouldn't loosen.

I grunted and swore as the car rental employee stood to the side, watching me as if I were a zoo animal.

"I ... just ... can't ... get ... it ... unhooked," I said, yanking furiously on the strap and sweating like an Arizona Diamondbacks mascot in July.

"I'd help but I don't have any kids," he mumbled, and honestly, I didn't blame him. I do have kids and I still can't figure it out.

But that's technology: Occasionally helpful, but just as often, annoying.

I mean, ask a kid.

Children have the reputation for aptitude when it comes to technology, but watch a 5-year-old try to use a desktop computer and see exactly how skilled they really are.

My son has many times gotten frustrated trying to pull up a video to watch on our computer.

He'll tap the screen, assuring me it's broken.

Because technology has tricked him, and now he thinks every screen is a touch screen.

But technology gets the best of us all. I'm now a person who requires my phone to remember every phone number — from my dad's to the pizza place we order from once a week.

We used to store that information in our heads, but that was before our memories withered in technology's sun.

Now, technology isn't all bad. You can fast-forward through commercials, use an app to find lost keys and conduct a work meeting without ever having to put on pants.

But, as with all technology, there are tradeoffs.

We just have to remember that no matter how good technology gets, we — our brains and our bodies — are the most high-tech gadgets we own.

I mean, if nothing else, we always have a neck to fall back on.

Smoking's Long, Slow Slide Into Oblivion

May 27, 2023

  It's become common at the start of movies and TV shows to show a list of all the various ways the content contained therewithin is inappropriate for children.

  You're warned about any stray cursing and sexual activity, violence and self-harm, but the one that always blows me away is the warning about smoking. It's shocking — not because smoking is good for you or because kids should smoke — but because it reminds me that there is no activity that has undergone more of a transformation in the mind of Americans than smoking has.

  In the span of my (relatively short, so far) life, smoking's reputation has gone to the dogs. Smoking used to be shorthand for coolness, the most certain way to transmit a character's blase insouciance toward life's harsh realities.

  Yes, cigarettes might kill you, the 1980s smoker seemed to say, *but so what?*

  There was a time, earlier than that, even, when heroes smoked — John Wayne and Humphrey Bogart — but by my day, it had been reduced to the domain of bad guys, tough women, teenagers and other rebels.

  Though we didn't live in the cloud of smoke that writer Fran Lebowitz said was the norm in her day, there was still plenty of smoking. I remember one TWA flight from New York to Greece as a child where there were so many smokers on board that, upon exiting the plane, my best use would have been topping a bagel with cream cheese.

In the decades since, however, the act of smoking has become so shocking, so beyond the pale that even villains don't do it. Kids in 2023 could be forgiven for thinking that no one in the entire world — hero or villain — smokes. They don't see smoking at restaurants, in offices or even outside, and now they don't see it on TV, either.

I smoked cigarettes myself, for a while, though I did it with aggressive casualness. I never woke up in the morning and smoked a cigarette, and I could go for days or even weeks without one if I felt sick. I quit because smoking wasn't fun enough to risk dying over, and it was too expensive to justify.

But there was something about a cigarette — the deep breathing, I guess — and there are times even now when I occasionally long for a smoke. I felt particularly antsy during the first presidential debate between Joe Biden and Donald Trump, and threatened to my husband that if things continued in their unhinged fashion, I would drive to the gas station and break decades of abstinence.

I have kids of my own now, though, and that more than anything has kept me from being truly tempted. I remember finding my own father's cigarettes when I was 9 years old. I knew enough to know that they were bad for him, and I nicked the pack from the console of his truck and stuffed them under the seat.

I didn't want him to die, and smoking seemed like the most dangerous thing he could do. When you're young, your parents are majestic, and anything that can bring them down feels like pretty foul stuff.

As an adult, smoking still isn't worth anyone's suffering.

Plus, the destruction of smoking's reputation in this country isn't a mixed bag. As a public health measure, the elimination of public smoking has been a phenomenal success. As a simple reduction in the annoyances we face — seeing cigarette butts everywhere and coming home from bars reeking — it's an improvement as well.

In the end, smoking's metamorphosis is strange but fine. I may notice smoking's absence, but I don't miss it much.

Good riddance to bad habits, I suppose.

I've Exited Lactation Station. Now Please Tell My Doctors

July 1, 2023

I am not breastfeeding.

I feel compelled to share that information because many people continue to labor under the misbelief that I, a 40-plus-year-old woman who last bore a child more than 5 years ago, am breastfeeding.

Each time I go to the pharmacist, the person behind the counter will, just as they're about to hand over my prescribed medication, grip it a bit tighter, pull it back and give me a look I've come to understand.

"I can't give you this," they say. "You're lactating."

Primarily, I object to the term, which focuses more on the process than the end result — the breastfeeding — and makes me sound like a leaky faucet.

But, also, I am not lactating.

My final foray into lactating culminated a short period of time after the birth of my youngest child, when I took my breast pumps and nipple ointment, breast shields and nipple guards, and put them into a bag.

I did not do what I wanted to do with that material, which was send it up on the next rocket full of billionaires headed into outer space with firm instructions for them to fire it into the sun.

Instead, I tried to pawn it off on someone else.

For a woman who breastfed for such a short period of time, I had a ridiculous amount of accessories. I even had car adapters for my breast pumps with the kind of shields that go under your clothes so you can have the dubious pleasure of lactating while driving 70 mph down the highway.

But you can't sell that stuff. You can't even give it away.

Apparently, no one wants something that had your bodily fluids — no matter how nutritious — coursing through it. I had to throw it all away, and I did it years ago.

But thanks to some apparently immovable notation in my medical file, I continue to be a breastfeeding mother, at least officially, even up to the point at which my youngest child enters primary school.

Not that there aren't some women who breastfeed — and happily — for as long as they think I'm keeping it up. I've got firsthand evidence, in fact.

As a young reporter, I was conducting an interview with a woman about a topic unrelated to lactating as her children played before us.

Suddenly, her daughter — a child fully 4 years old if she was a day — ran up, yanked down her mother's shirt and began breastfeeding.

The woman gave a deep sigh and shot me a look.

Preschoolers, it seemed to say.

I was horrified.

Not that I had or have a problem with the female body, and I certainly believe mothers should be free to breastfeed whenever and wherever they like.

But the idea that, when I had a child, my body would belong so completely to another being that the person would feel free to spontaneously denude me in front of strangers conducting business? And that it would happen long past the time when said person became capable of tying her own shoes?

That scared me.

But when I had my kids, I felt the pressure that nearly

every mother knows: The Pressure to Be Perfect.

And a perfect mother sure as heck breastfeeds.

So, I ate lactation cookies and saw lactation consultants. I took fenugreek and did breast massages. I laughed at the articles saying that to get more milk, I had to get more sleep. I did it all.

But now, I'm done with it. All of it. Thank God.

The only final hurdle is to get that "lactating" note removed from my file. So, I patiently remind the pharmacist each time, and every time I visit a doctor, I ask them to change the notation from "lactater" to "former lactater."

No matter how many tries it takes, I'm gonna make it happen. I just know it.

Because if I can lactate, I can do anything.

The Wild, Weird History of Pets in My House

July 8, 2023

This Fourth of July, social media was abuzz with fireworks complaints — not due to parents bemoaning the awakening of sleeping babies, but from pet owners upset by how their dogs had been scarred by the noise.

All the chatter got me thinking about how my husband and I don't have any pets, nor do we have any plans or desire to get one.

We're a non-pet house, a rarity these days, with rates of pet ownership eclipsing the rates of people with children in their homes. Our kids occasionally mention pets, but thus far, we've resisted. For one reason, look no further than the tangled and bizarre history of pets in my household growing up.

The first pets I remember having were fish, and I remember them chiefly because of an incident in which my 4-year-old brother smashed our fish tank with a toy mallet, sending sprays of saltwater and tropical sea creatures out over our living room carpet.

"The fish are dying!" I wailed to my parents as they frantically scooped the fish into soup cans and cups full of tap water.

As a child, I pitied the fish. As an adult, I pity the parents.

The fish were followed by an exotic bird my dad got after

a job on an oil freighter. When he repaired their generator, the Brazilian sailors must have paid their bill at least partially in parrot, for my dad came home that day with a wide grin and the most beautiful bird I'd ever seen.

The parrot was colorful both in its plumage and its language, we learned, after our efforts to teach it to say "hello" and "pretty birdie" were met solely by a stubborn fusillade of Portuguese curses.

When we asked my dad what the bird was screaming, he just grunted and refused to translate.

The bird also bit, and after it nipped my hand particularly hard one day, my dad sold the parrot for hundreds of dollars to someone who was either extremely foolish or a South American swear word aficionado with fingers made of steel.

The next pets to cycle in were a pair of gerbils that my parents had been assured were both male but, as we soon learned, were not.

Some very natural but still very horrible things happened quickly thereafter, as the gerbils displayed both the rapidity of their gestational cycle and a willingness to continue breeding despite the preexistence of multiple litters of nursing young. After the third round of back-to-back procreation, my dad separated the gerbil parents into nearby cages.

The male, in an admirable display of devotion to the furthering of his species, chewed through the side of his cage to reach the female. After that, the gerbils disappeared, and we got a rabbit. A single rabbit.

She was a snow-white female, and instead of pooping her delicate little ball-droppings out onto the ground, she conveniently used a litterbox. For a time, it seemed, she would be our perfect pet.

But the rabbit didn't like people, and whenever I tried to cuddle it, I'd feel its little heart hammering away inside its chest. One day, the rabbit ran out of an open door, throwing her fate to the wind rather than face the further affections of an 8-year-old human.

At that point, my parents gave up, and the rabbit was succeeded by a revolving door of cats from the pound. There was a Siamese kitten whose cruelty was exceeded only by its unrelenting diarrhea, and two cats so unremarkable we resorted to simply calling them "Black Cat" and "Gray Cat."

Throughout the Great Pet Experiment, we had one perfect pet: a gray tabby named Pebbles.

But the Pebbles of the world are rare, like hitting a pet jackpot, and for now, I'm not ready to play the odds.

Instead, I'll sit back and watch all of you, you brave pet owners who've gambled, and consider the day when we might deal ourselves in.

I'll just make sure to brush up on my Portuguese first.

Samsara and the Fine Art of Not Caring About Dirty Laundry

July 29, 2023

I've recently discovered a way to apply the karmic concept of samsara — the endless wheel of death and rebirth through which we all move — to solve a practical problem: namely, laundry.

For at least at my house, it's a never-ending cycle, ebbing and flowing like the tide but never truly finding completion.

That, however, I have decided is just fine, because that's the way laundry is intended to be. If it were ever done, it wouldn't be laundry. And if I were ever to wash, dry and fold all of it, I just wouldn't be me.

I assume there are other, perhaps more motivated people who promptly clean their clothes before they have a chance to erupt into a Mount Vesuvius of soiled linen, but I am not one of those people. It helps to tell myself that I am a writer and therefore an artist and am therefore held to a lower housekeeping standard.

"I'm a writer!" I say when I spy my son's hamper, resplendent with camp shirts and swimsuits and bath towels. "I don't have time for this. I must return to my art."

(Feel free to steal that for yourself. It works, whether your art is music, writing or sculpting with your kids' Play-Doh.)

Now, it took me a while to admit that to myself and even

longer to say it out loud to others, that I was a "writer." I'm fairly well-adjusted for a writer, which is another way of saying that I'm not that great of one, and it had always made me feel a little pretentious to consider myself any kind of artist at all.

Please don't get me wrong: I'm a better writer than average, for sure, perhaps even better than most. But there are above me higher tiers, and it seems the higher one gets in those writerly tiers, the odder one becomes.

Just as an example, Jonathan Franzen — widely accepted as one of the finest living American writers — has spent the last 25 years beefing, alternately, with Oprah Winfrey, cats, Jennifer Weiner, the Audubon Society and the practice of ending phone calls by saying "I love you."

Almost definitionally, someone who has so many words squatting in their brain that they have to evict some onto a page for another person to deal with is kind of ... strange.

And I've always wanted to be normal.

I can't put my finger on the exact root of that deep yearning, but maybe it has something to do with the night my parents sent me to my first sleepover with, instead of a sleeping bag, a neon-red flokati rug so heavy I could barely carry it.

But I have found in my adulthood that there's power in considering yourself an artist, even just a slightly above-average one, and being strange is more fun than it used to be when I was 8 years old lying on 20 pounds of wool at my first American slumber party.

Now I can find beauty in my uniqueness, poetry in my failings.

And in the wisdom of Eastern religions, I can find explanation (if not justification) for my inability to fully denude my basement floor of dirty clothes.

I've found a balance between artistry and normalcy, death and life, a full hamper and an empty one, and it swings between the two, forever, like a giant pendulum.

OK, so my artistry ceiling is a little lower than some, but that's fine. I'd rather *not* spend my days fighting with cat people about whether their pets are the nation's top ecological threat. And conversely, I may not ever have an Instagram-worthy house, tastefully and sparingly decorated in varying shades of gray. That's fine, too.

Because on the great wheel of life, I'm happy in mid-cycle, just like my laundry.

The Firing Squad

It's the Debate Over CRT That Divides Us, Not the Issue of Racism Itself

November 13, 2021

If the mere mention of the letters "CRT" turns you from a mild-mannered person into a frothing green monster, know that you are not alone.

For I, too, am now triggered into an Incredible Hulk-like transformation whenever I hear or read about CRT, or "critical race theory," for those of you who've been blissfully absent from our national conversation lately.

You might ask, "What, exactly, is critical race theory?" And that would be an excellent and thus-far-poorly answered question.

If you listen to conservatives (particularly those seeking election to public office), it's a deranged effort to lower white kids' self-esteem.

If you listen to liberals (particularly those who like to fact-check viral tweets), it's a postgraduate legal theory about systemic racism that *never* creeps into public education, in any form.

The source of my rage is the infuriating liberal response to conservative criticism of CRT. Liberals get sucked into definitional arguments and name-calling, letting the wedge issue do its work. Instead, let's talk about this: We don't want to raise racist kids.

Unless you are an objectively bad caregiver, you're looking for ways to encourage kindness, empathy and fairness. You want children to view others as worthy of respect — no matter their skin color.

The problem, though, is that for decades, parents and caregivers of white children have tried to accomplish that by avoiding talking about race. We've done it with the best intentions, trying to raise our children to be "colorblind," but research has shown that not discussing race doesn't help kids overcome their biases.

Instead, we need to explain to them that no, they're not blind — people do have different skin tones, but they should not make value judgements based on those skin tones.

It's seemingly simple but parents often find it challenging, either because they don't know what to say or because they're harboring racial resentment of their own.

But schools cannot encourage mistreatment of some of their students at the benefit of the innocence of the others. Educators must discuss race.

(Too) many years ago, I attended school in New Orleans, at a school with a racially and economically diverse student body and teaching staff. My fifth-grade teacher, Mrs. Hall, was a robust and cheerful woman, and I still vividly remember the sadness in her voice as she described to us how, when she was our age, she had asked her mother to go into a diner downtown.

"No, sorry, honey," she was told. "They don't serve Black people."

When I got home, I ran to ask my mother:

"Is that true? Did they really not let Black people eat in some restaurants?"

My mom nodded, and I cried, not for Mrs. Hall but for a girl my age, who'd been heartbroken years before.

Now, did Mrs. Hall indoctrinate me? Should she have left that conversation to my mother, who had never previously discussed race? Should I have had interactions with other kids in my class without knowing anything about their lives as Black people?

That's not to say that the topic of anti-racism isn't

complicated.

Almost all of us have been in diversity and inclusion training sessions of questionable value, where no one's mind was opened and no one's opinion changed. And we've all heard tales of overreach, cases where divisions were sowed instead of healed.

Liberals do no one any favors by failing to acknowledge that there are honest complaints about some diversity, equity and inclusion efforts. Not everyone who questions the efficacy or fairness of these efforts is a racist.

We must move past all the arguing over definitions, and the parsing of what is and what isn't CRT, into the important questions: Is anti-racist training good? Does it work?

Because ignoring race shouldn't (and can't) be the answer.

Conservatives Can't Help Capitalizing On Gun Tragedies

December 11, 2021

It's the holidays, and a school shooter recently stole the lives of four Michigan children, so, naturally, some consider it the perfect time for assault rifle jokes.

Rep. Thomas Massie of Kentucky and Rep. Lauren Boebert of Colorado both recently tweeted family Christmas cards showing themselves and their kids posing with assault weapons, raising the bile of millions and succeeding at transparent ploys for attention.

There used to be a time when, after a school shooting, GOP politicians and lobbyists would mostly stay quiet, claiming it was "too soon" to talk about our increasingly lax gun laws, postponing any action.

They knew that delays served as opportunities for lobbyists to intervene, for gun makers to dispense money, for pundits to prevaricate, for politicians to lie — and that by the time it was deemed appropriate to discuss whether we should allow anyone to have and carry anywhere as many guns of as many types as they wanted, well, by the time we got around to that conversation, the sharp tang of grief would have faded for all except those who'd watched the bodies of their children be lowered into the ground.

GOP politicians and lobbyists knew that, after such a delay, they might hide that a majority in our country favor more gun restrictions and two-thirds of Americans don't even own a gun. They knew they could ignore that law enforcement organizations want limits on the types of guns people can own and where they can bring them. They knew they could distract from the fact that making limitless amounts of high-powered, high-capacity weapons available to everyone *threatens* everyone — even (or perhaps especially) the guns' owners themselves.

Once the "too soon" time had passed, the outrage machine would've moved on to a new topic (hopefully, from their view, some juicy culture war squabble) and the lives lost, needlessly taken at the altar of gun worship, would be forgotten.

Now, though, there is no longer even a brief pause in nasty rhetoric after a school shooting.

The corporate benefactors of increasing gun sales, and the pundits and politicians they've purchased with their blood money, have been emboldened.

They know they've fully won the war against even minor, reasonable gun restrictions. The National Rifle Association and other lobbyists have properly fleeced rational gun owners in their quest to remove all rules and limitations, and their money has done its job. They have bought politicians who have installed judges who will no longer even entertain the thought that the framers of the Constitution perhaps did not envision the existence of a gun so powerful it could shoot 150 bullets per minute through a metal door.

That conversation has concluded.

Conservative politicians and pundits no longer feel the need to address why it's traumatic for children to wear masks at school but not for kids as young as 5 to hide under their desks in preparatory active shooter drills.

As a nation, we now skip even the most rudimentary mourning and rocket directly into the kinds of assaults on good taste that Massie and Boebert perpetrated.

They should feel shame, but instead they feel only a cheap

thrill from needling their political opponents.

It's a cheap thrill because, like a drug, the high is transitory. They will need more, soon, and more and more of it to fill the hole they've dug in their own hearts, the hole they've created where compassion should be.

To paraphrase Christopher Hitchens, the orator and writer who died almost exactly 10 years ago: Even if you don't believe in hell, some people give you reason to wish there were one for them to go to.

Meet the GOP of 2022: Snowflakes and Safe Spaces

January 15, 2022

When I was a little girl, a neighbor friend came to me one day, telling me her mom had forbidden her to play with me anymore.

She'd learned, you see, that I had She-Ra dolls and, as the girl told me, "She-Ra uses magic."

They were conservative Evangelical Christians, as were we, and I went to my mom, sad and confused about what had happened.

"When someone is insecure in what they believe," my mom explained, "then sometimes they want to stay away from other beliefs completely. They're worried they might not be able to resist the different idea."

I can't help thinking about that recently, learning that the GOP announced their presidential candidates will have to sign a promise not to debate Democrats in any events held by the Commission on Presidential Debates, a nonpartisan group.

There's something deep about Republicans refusing to even debate Democrats anymore.

One particular complaint the GOP had with the current system was that moderators have, in real time, fact-checked politicians like Mitt Romney and Donald Trump. It's not fair, apparently, to have your lies called out on national TV.

It's just the latest move in the conservative retreat to safe spaces.

Republican senators have successfully wooed "Democratic" Sen. Joe Manchin and "Democratic" Sen. Kyrsten Sinema into keeping alive the filibuster, a Senate rule that requires a supermajority vote to pass most legislation. The threat of a filibuster means no law can pass without a Republican's agreement.

Republican Senate Minority Leader Mitch McConnell, who previously had no problem with changing Senate rules when he was the one doing the alteration, touts the filibuster as the character of the Senate, which is, I guess, technically true as it exists solely to protect corrupt politicians who want to kill popular legislation if it goes against their naked self-interest.

Sinema recently said that, though she supported the voting rights bill Democrats were trying to pass, she couldn't support something that would cause political divisions.

One wonders if, upon seeing someone breaking into her house, Sinema would call 911 to report the crime, a divisive move if I ever heard of one.

Then there are the anti-critical race theory laws popping up like weeds in every red state in the nation — laws intended to prevent teachers from teaching anything that might make a conservative uncomfortable, sad or angry. Even Nazis can't be maligned anymore, according to one Indiana lawmaker who later walked back his strange comments alleging Nazism and fascism shouldn't be judged right or wrong by teachers.

How does someone allege they're against "cancel culture" but are fine with the cancellation of a teacher who says slavery is wrong?

Conservatives now must like every question from the press, must support every law that's passed, must agree with every word that's ever spoken to their child. Quite a turnaround for a political party that once held sacred the idea that feelings aren't facts, life is tough and that sometimes you should stop complaining, suck it up and play the hand you're dealt.

Today's Republican politicians cannot have their voters be exposed to opposing viewpoints, hear a foul word spoken against their political party or even learn the history of those who share their race, their gender or their religion.

Maybe they're worried they'll wilt in the glare of criticism.

More likely, though, they're like the mom of that friend I used to have, worried that the other ideas out there are more persuasive than their own. They fear the weakness of their arguments.

For there's no one who hollers as loudly, who bangs the drum more fiercely, who attacks with more violence, than someone who's worried they might be wrong.

Leprechauns? Fine. Two Dads? Too Far

April 16, 2022

I was driving my kids to their swimming lessons the other day when I listened, a bit amused and a bit horrified, as disagreement escalated into full-fledged debate over what they clearly considered a crucial point of contention: Do leprechauns wear brown boots or black?

They agreed that leprechauns always wear green clothes (of course) but, in addition to the boot issue, sparred on whether we can't see leprechauns because they're too small or because they're too quick.

"What's the truth, Mommy?" my older son asked.

Instead of answering with the truth truth, something on par with, "I have failed as a parent," I dodged:

"I don't know. I've never seen a leprechaun."

My kids learned about leprechauns, obviously, in school, the same place they learned about elves (on shelves) and the tooth fairy.

They haven't stopped talking, or arguing, about any of them, and I find myself marveling at how, in many places, it's perfectly acceptable for teachers to instruct on the existence of fake Christmas sweatshop employees but not on real life — people who actually exist and events that actually took place.

It's not OK to teach history anymore (if it's something that makes anyone feel guilty or sad) and it's not acceptable to talk about anyone being gay or trans because, apparently, admitting that some men marry men is worse than vividly describing the plot of "Fifty Shades of Grey." Science is too controversial, and not even a teacher with a master's degree is allowed to question the beliefs of parents who think vaccines make you magnetic.

Perfectly fine in school, however, is asking kids how much the tooth fairy brought them for their first tooth. Thanks to that instructional topic, I now have a bone to pick with the parents of one of my son's classmates, who gave their child a $100 bill for losing a tooth.

"Does the tooth fairy always give $100?" my son asked in amazement.

"No, she most certainly does not," I replied firmly.

Thankfully, someone else (maybe a fellow classmate, who even knows anymore) told him an absurd story about the tooth fairy using the smuggled teeth to build a giant castle.

"That must have been a super important piece of the castle," my son said, justifying the largess.

"Exactly. A cornerstone piece, maybe."

I then had to explain what a cornerstone is, which was fine — good, even. If he's going to learn about mythical tooth-hoarders, maybe I can sneak in some facts along with it.

And facts should be on the curriculum, don't you think?

My younger son came home from preschool and recounted several facts about his classmates: one has a peanut allergy; another has two dads. A third threw up on the table and the teachers had to move everyone, even though I'm told it still smelled from the other side of the room.

These are facts. They wouldn't bother me as school topics even if I had a problem with gay marriage, because the idea that my 3-year-old has any clue what being married sometimes entails (if you're lucky, and you've already put the kids to bed and done the dishes and laundry and you have any energy left) is laughable.

Now, not every parent who wants teachers to avoid

contentious topics is a bigot, and you can be forgiven for worrying that kids are susceptible.

But every day our children encounter, in forms both benign and foul, topics we may wish they didn't. And some of those lessons are less delicately delivered than we would hope.

But that's pretty much life, isn't it?

If we can't handle the thought that our children will learn about this messy, gorgeous world, thanks to, or, in spite of us, well, homeschooling's always an option.

But in public schools, and on TikTok, and from their babysitters and friends, they learn all kinds of fiction.

Shouldn't they, sometimes, be exposed to facts, as well?

For Parents, Baby Formula Is More Than Food. It's a Lifeline

May 21, 2022

When I finally gave up on what had been both a herculean and a Sisyphean effort to breastfeed, resigning my lanolin and breast pump to mere props in my nightmares, I wanted to know more about alternatives to breastfeeding.

I asked my dad, who grew up in the mountains of Greece with no electricity and no weekly pediatrician visits, what did village women who couldn't breastfeed do?

I'd heard from innumerable breastfeeding evangelists how natural it is, how any woman can do it, how you can even breastfeed if you didn't give birth (if you only try hard enough and take enough medication). But after having been through it, seeing my children scream in pain after drinking my breast milk and never get enough to fill their tiny bellies, I knew that as far back as humanity has gone, there would have been others like me.

What did they do?

"Oh, yes," my dad said, as if pulling up a memory he hadn't accessed in decades. "The women used to boil rice in goat's milk, then strain it."

If those uneducated women, like my grandmother, who never completed the fourth grade, knew that recipe, then of course they knew the necessity for it. They must have known that sometimes breastfeeding couldn't work, or wouldn't be best for mother or child.

As ignorant as they were, they knew more than some of us, who still claim that there is no insurmountable barrier to breastfeeding.

And as an infant formula shortage empties store shelves, and parents struggle to feed their children, there's been far too much gloating about how this might push women back toward breastfeeding and away from formula.

For my part, I struggled for months with breastfeeding both of my children. The trouble with my first son began almost immediately.

I quickly was told to start something called "triple feeding," a hellish process in which the mother breastfeeds, then bottle feeds, then uses a breast pump. Sometimes the second category of bottle feeding was broken up into two parts: pumped breast milk and formula supplementation.

Since newborns eat once every two hours, and the process sometimes took up to an hour and 45 minutes, it is no exaggeration to say that virtually all of my time in those early days was consumed.

I stashed food near the rocking chair I used to feed and pump, bought a portable breast pump with a car adapter, and used special shields for the pump that fit inside my bra so that I could even pump milk while driving or doing laundry.

I won't list the other reasons why we moved from breast milk to formula. Frankly, it upsets me to think I ever felt it necessary to justify it, to myself or anyone else.

Simply, the answer is this: Baby formula fed my children, but it saved my life.

In a time of postpartum desperation, Formula swooped in, patted my head and told me not to worry.

"I got this," Formula told me.

When I think of new mothers now, many still struggling with the guilt from using formula, or parents who never had another choice, I know the loss of formula will be more than just another supply chain disruption. It will be a disruption to their happiness, to their safety, to their very existence.

And though some emergency measures are being taken, if politicians value babies and mothers the way they claim to, they will ensure that such disruption never happens again.

They will help expand production, eliminate near-monopolies in the industry and remove obstacles to accessing safe imported formula.

The importance of enacting these changes cannot be overstated.

It is a matter, quite literally, of life or death.

Do we care enough to act?

For the millions of mothers like me, I desperately hope so.

Student Loan Forgiveness Is Deranging Republican Politicians

August 27, 2022

Our country is suffering through a gigantic Republican freakout right now, one precipitated by the news that President Joe Biden has announced the student loan forgiveness of up to $20,000 per borrower.

The freakout — let's call it "Student Loan Derangement Syndrome" -- has taken several forms.

Chief among them are the over-the-top predictions that the move will lead to catastrophic consequences to the middle class, to our economy — even to national security.

As just one example, Rep. Jim Banks of Indiana (R, obviously) tweeted that forgiving student loans was bad because it would make military recruitment harder.

Now, it's true that some go into the military because they are poor and can't otherwise afford college, but, and I can't believe I have to say this, that is not a good thing.

That's like saying we should end seat-belt laws to increase organ donation or arguing that food pantries are bad because they lead to fewer blood donations.

Poor people are not a natural resource.

Then there are the hypocrites, never in short supply but particularly plentiful of late.

Republican Reps. Marjorie Taylor Greene and Matt Gaetz were up in arms about the announcement but seem to have no problem with loan forgiveness as a general concept. They both took out and were forgiven tens of thousands of dollars in payroll protection loans during the pandemic.

They, and plenty of other critics of Biden's move, have passionate but strikingly newfound moral objections to borrowing money from the government and then not paying it back.

There's also an outbreak of "pay-your-own-way-ism" infecting Republicans.

To them, tax cuts, corporate welfare and subsidies to coal companies, giant farming conglomerates and drug manufacturers aren't examples of situations where people should pay their own way.

Paying your own way means taking out $100,000 in student loans and then working at whatever grim job you can get for the privilege of making continued payments on those loans.

Republican Sen. Mitt Romney worries that loan forgiveness "creates irresponsible expectations."

Now, when I went to college (redacted) years ago, I felt quite keenly the unfairness of having to put myself into debt to pay for a degree that helped me more in the title than it did in the education. My husband helped me repay my student loans. Maybe Romney thinks I should have turned him down.

"No," I should have said, "I need to pay my own way. How will I ever learn responsible expectations otherwise?"

I'm assuming Romney's kids have never gotten so much as a free lollipop out of the fear that it will create entitlement issues.

Meanwhile, Donald Trump's social media company owes $1.6 million to creditors and reportedly hasn't paid the bills since March. But that's different to conservatives because those weren't loans; they were contractually agreed-upon charges. And they're not being forgiven; they're just not being paid back.

Now, let's admit that there are good arguments against forgiving student loans: It doesn't benefit non-college-educated people and it doesn't do anything to solve the underlying problem with higher education, which is that college costs far too much and confers degrees of questionable value.

But Republicans aren't making good arguments. They're taking wild, random jabs, mostly because they realize how popular the decision will be.

Rank populism has been their purview, and now that a Democratic president is engaging in it, suddenly they see its dangers.

If conservatives want to debate student loan forgiveness, fine. Let's debate it. But let's debate in good faith, without the histrionics, hyperbole and hypocrisy. Let's not debate just because the plan's proponents have Ds after their names instead of Rs.

Because that's not discussion. It's derangement. And we shouldn't forgive that.

Who's the Queen? (And Other Fake Questions That Were Never Asked)

September 10, 2022

The following is a wholly fabricated, fictitious conversation between a college professor and his students on Sept. 8, 2022, shortly after the Royal Family announced the death of Queen Elizabeth II.

TEACHER: Class, I have bad news for you all. We've just learned that someone tremendously influential has died.

STUDENT A: Oh, no! From TikTok or from Instagram?

TEACHER: (Deep sigh) No, not a *social media* influencer. An influential person. The queen. The queen has died.

CLASS IN UNISON: Queen Latifah died???

TEACHER: Not Queen Latifah. Queen Elizabeth II of England.

STUDENT B: Oh. How old was she?

TEACHER: She was 96, and she lived a full life, that's true. But she was of tremendous importance to her people, and her advanced age actually rendered her death even more unbelievable. Because she had lived for so long, many began to take for granted that she would never die.

STUDENT A: So, you're saying the queen was, like, Betty White, and the rest of the world was, like, People magazine?

TEACHER: She was a little more important to world

history than Betty White.

STUDENT C: Why? Was she the boss of England or something?

TEACHER: She didn't rule, no. The monarch in the United Kingdom holds a mostly ceremonial position. But she was queen during all of the wonderful and terrible moments of most Britons' lives, and she publicly represented them at innumerable important occasions and cultural events. They saw her face everywhere — on their money and on their stamps — and sang "God Save the Queen" at sporting events. She was sort of ... Great Britain's mascot.

STUDENT C: Like Uga.

TEACHER: Who's Uga?

STUDENT C: The bulldog that goes to all the University of Georgia football games. It's their mascot. People really love that dog.

TEACHER: No, she was nothing at all like Uga. The queen was an enduring symbol of the United Kingdom, and she held the position for 70 years, longer than any other British monarch. People all over the world are grieving her loss, including here in our own country.

STUDENT C: In the United States? But didn't we fight a war so we wouldn't have to bow down to their kings and queens? I'm pretty sure Lin-Manuel Miranda wrote a whole musical about it.

TEACHER: Yes, she's not our queen, but she also symbolized more than just the job she did. To many, her name and the continuation of the monarchy represented stability, dignity, devotion to duty ...

STUDENT D: Hundreds of years of violent colonial oppression against people in Ireland, India and throughout the Caribbean and Africa, just to name a few places?

TEACHER: Well ... maybe that, too. But we should remember that, while the dead have no feelings, those they left behind do. She seems to have been a good person, gentle and thoughtful, by all accounts, and beloved by many. She was a mother, a grandmother and a great-grandmother. Her family is mourning her right now, and that's important to keep in mind.

STUDENT A: Plus, she was famous.

TEACHER: Yes, extremely famous. Think of the most famous person you know.

STUDENT A: Zendaya.

TEACHER: Famous but British.

STUDENT B: Harry Styles.

TEACHER: Famous for something other than being attractive.

STUDENT C: Donald Trump.

TEACHER: Maybe it's time to move on. Let's get started on that quiz I told you we were having today.

STUDENT E: Sir, I need the day off to mourn. My great-grandparents were mostly British, and my mom just texted me that in the queen's remembrance, we're all going to watch "The Crown," lose at soccer and put vinegar on our fries.

TEACHER: Class dismissed.

The New Beatitudes

September 17, 2022

Blessed art the millionaires, for a million dollars does not goeth as far as it used to.

Blessed art the governors of Florida and Texas, for they owneth the libs in the most Christlike way possible when they droppeth off desperate migrants, starving and exhausted, in blue cities for publicity stunts, treating human beings as props in political theater.

Blessed art those who are still posting pictures of the pump at the gas station after they filleth up.

Blessed art those who, every time it snows, sarcastically ask, "Whatever happened to global warming?"

Blessed art those who took federal payment protection loans, asked for those loans to be forgiven and now complain about student loan forgiveness.

Blessed art the senators, the congressmen, the radio and TV hosts, the pundits, the LibsofTikTokkers and the tweeters serving on the culture wars' front lines. For, lo, they do labor for one goal only, and that is the betterment of mankind. It hath nothing to do with book sales, cushy consultant gigs, speaking fees and "gifts" from lobbyists.

Blessed art the CEOs, the Randian conservatives and the

corporate communications flaks, for it becometh increasingly difficult to find ways to complain about low unemployment rates in the United States.

Blessed art the victims of cancel culture, people punished for following their beliefs, unless those people were Republican politicians who did not believe the election was stolen, in which case, those RINOs got what was coming to them. People fired for offensive tweets are martyrs of Christ, but teachers fired for admitting they're gay should've just kept their mouths shut.

Blessed art those who "Back The Blue" unless The Blue are FBI agents lawfully executing a search warrant.

Blessed art the gun-nuts, for "The Prince of Peace" would be a great name for an assault rifle, and endless murders of children are a small price to pay for unimpeded access to military-grade weaponry.

Blessed art those who said one person should be imprisoned for having non-classified information on a personal email server but have no problem with someone keeping nuclear secrets in a room at a golf resort.

Blessed art those who fervently believe that someone should make their own medical decisions when it comes to COVID vaccines and masking, but not when it comes to pregnancy or gender transition.

Blessed art the New Feminists, people who would once have called someone a "hairy-legged trout" for suggesting that anything has ever been even slightly more difficult for women. But, lo, these New Feminists hath discovered a burgeoning passion for reproductive rights, women's sports and woman-centric language when (and only when) it concerns transgender issues.

Blessed art the victims of reverse racism, any white person who suffers a negative consequence that they believeth should instead have been vested upon a person of color.

Blessed art the truth-seekers, the red-faced hyperventilators, for they valiantly uncovereth conspiracies about lizard people, pizza-parlor satanists and JFK Jr.'s whereabouts. That they happen to also be making millions of dollars from the credulous and the fearful is a complete coincidence, and The Lord Our God resents the inference that they art vile con men.

Blessed art those who oppose federal minimum wage increases, paid maternity leave, improvements to veterans' benefits and health care subsidies, for now they complaineth about how hard it is to get good help these days.

Blessed art those who refuse help to the poor, saying they will always be with us, knowing that, therefore, thou needest feel no obligation to care for them.

And though thou may be tempted otherwise — for selfishness and hypocrisy often are the partners of fame, wealth and other transitory rewards — instead rejoice and be glad if thou art not so thoroughly blessed as these kinds of men.

For, truly, it is those without these blessings who will inherit the Kingdom of Heaven.

Can Anything Stop the Wave of Conservative Fury?

November 5, 2022

I dreamed last night that I watched bombs explode outside my house, missiles dropped from planes flying high in the sky.

As the bombs landed, pieces of debris flew toward me. It occurred to me that I knew who had attacked us: It was not a foreign enemy, but fellow Americans who had bombed our neighborhood.

"The bombs are from another state, a red state," I remember thinking, as if that made total sense, that a Republican state would attack us merely for being a Democratic one.

In the nightmare, I screamed for my husband to grab the kids and tried to rush upstairs to them. I could not find them. As my panic rose, suddenly I woke up, covered in sweat.

I realized, as my heart returned to its normal rhythm, that my dream was about the midterms.

What can I say about the midterm election other than that politics have become so vicious, so cruel that we have become inured to the very real signs of increasing political violence.

Paul Pelosi, husband of Rep. Nancy Pelosi, recently was attacked in his home, reportedly by a man who told police he was trying to find and hurt the speaker of the House. According to police, the man had built an extensive online presence full of right-wing conspiracy theories.

Afterward, instead of expressing horror at the attack and considering the role the GOP played in inspiring political violence, the conservative smear machine started a new conspiracy theory, that the attacker was Paul Pelosi's lover. People like Donald Trump Jr. mocked the incident on social media and other prominent conservatives suggested Pelosi or the Democrats were to blame.

Meanwhile, in Arizona, so-called election-monitoring groups only recently were prevented from showing up to ballot boxes openly armed, lying about election laws and recording voters dropping off ballots. In a hearing about the group's actions, one man told the judge that he and his wife were harassed, and their information publicly blasted out by GOP showman Steve Bannon, who called them ballot mules.

On the opposite side of the country, a video recently went viral of a Baptist pastor talking about how he'd seen a boy wearing fingernail polish. The pastor told his flock that he was shocked the kid "looked like a boy" otherwise.

"I'm just like, oh, I want to break his fingers," the pastor said, from the pulpit.

In Oklahoma, a man wearing what looked a lot like a MAGA hat threw a Molotov cocktail through the window of a donut shop after they hosted a drag show. He left an anti-LGBT letter on a neighboring business.

And those are just the happenings of the last week or so.

So, do I feel targeted by conservatives, merely for political differences? Do I know some Republicans think their beliefs should be enforced at the end of a gun? Even though my nightmare is clearly impossible, do I think it represents a metaphor for the very real anger surging through the GOP?

I suppose I do.

I suppose I don't feel like someone conservatives simply disagree with.

The GOP has called liberals like me murderers for supporting abortion rights, groomers for favoring LGBT rights, Nazis for believing in gun control and fascists for considering the 2020 election legal and fair.

My unconscious mind might be forgiven, therefore, for mistaking the midterms for a civil war.

I can wish it were otherwise, wish that the temperature might be lowered and the fires of passion dampened, but at the same time I can know that it doesn't seem very likely.

My only hope is that, after the midterms, the insanity will stop — for a little while, at least.

There is, after all, 2024 coming up.

A New Expert Is Born Every Second

December 10, 2022

Our country is now an expert factory.

We churn them out left and right, and the machines that produce them on every topic — from international diplomacy to the inner workings of giant companies — run, now, seemingly nonstop.

The foreign policy expert machine chugged to life recently, after President Joe Biden announced a deal releasing basketball star Brittney Griner from a Russian labor camp in a trade for Russian arms dealer Viktor Bout.

Our newly minted experts, including Donald Trump Jr., criticized Biden for not securing the release of ex-Marine Paul Whelan instead of Griner. No matter that Whelan had been convicted of espionage, a much more serious crime. No matter that U.S. officials said Whelan's release was never a possibility, no matter that two very different presidents have been unable to get Whelan out and no matter that Whelan had already been passed over in a prisoner exchange with Russia earlier this year.

The foreign policy experts have spoken!

It has come to the attention of several thousand Facebook commenters (who have, it must be admitted, no experience negotiating the release of political prisoners) an error was made. The president's advisers, with their decades of public service, education and training? Well, let's just say they could learn from Bob, a CPA in Tacoma who watches a lot of CNN.

Somehow, our country's Bobs magically divined the content of the secret negotiations between the U.S. and Russia and therefore know exactly how they, personally, could have gotten a better outcome.

Brand-new media experts started rolling off the factory line this week, too, after the publication of "The Twitter Files."

If you haven't heard of "The Twitter Files" because you aren't on Twitter, or don't care about Elon Musk, or don't enjoy reading boring internal corporate emails, you are forgiven.

Basically, "The Twitter Files" is an attempt to prove that there was favoritism on Twitter to liberals.

The proof? Emails showing both Republicans and Democrats, including officials in both the Trump and Biden teams, reaching out to alert Twitter officials to tweets they thought were problematic.

That might seem benign, but that's not all!

Twitter also, apparently, pushed down content and made it harder to find users who posted problematic tweets. (We should, I suppose, ignore the fact that Twitter warns in its terms of service that those tactics might be used on offensive tweets or users.)

On top of that, a Twitter lawyer with ties to the Biden administration was reading the emails before they were sent to the "Twitter Files" journalists. A lawyer! Just think!

Now, I came out of the media expert factory some time ago, so you'll have to excuse me if I'm confused at what, exactly, was so alarming about all of this.

Lawyers read plenty of the stories I wrote in my years at newspapers. I would have trouble counting the times someone powerful reached out to try to get me to downplay or boost a story. Media companies decline every day to promote objectionable content.

But what do I know? The Bobs have spoken: "The Twitter Files" are a bombshell.

There is a certain democracy in this new landscape, one in which anyone can comment on anything. We're all experts, if we wish to be, and we all have a shot at having our voices heard.

Opinions are fine — healthy, even. For as long as there have been societies, there has been discourse. And every child thinks their parents don't know what they're talking about. But as you get older, we learn the value of experience and wisdom.

The trouble comes when the army of Bobs start believing they really do know better than the actual experts, and acting as if that were true. Bob is not a hostage negotiator, a doctor, a scientist, a CEO, a diplomat.

Question? Yes. Opine? Absolutely.

But we should all understand our limitations, acknowledge where a real expert might know better than a factory-fresh one.

Because, Bob? I'm sure you're an expert on something. Just probably not on that.

High Egg Prices Really Are Just Chicken Scratch

January 21, 2023

Everyone's complaining about how expensive eggs have gotten lately, but I haven't been stressing.

I've always bought the extra-pricey eggs anyway, the ones with the drawings of flowers on them, the ones that promise the chickens who laid your eggs were raised on a bucolic farm in Iowa where each hen gets her own house, the chicks are taken for twice-daily walks in tiny perambulators and a trained avian masseuse visits every week to give them a nice Swedish rubdown.

Why do I pay more? I haven't seen any horrible documentaries about factory farming, and it's not like I have money to burn. It's just that I've known plenty of chickens in my time and they're mostly a decent sort.

There *was* that one rooster who ruled my grandparents' henhouse, the one who, when I was 3 years old, chased me around the yard mercilessly. Each time he caught me, he'd peck me viciously, as if attacking a threat to his masculine dominion. One day, he pushed his luck too far, though. Deciding he'd nipped his last toddler, my grandmother dispensed the Greek version of frontier justice, lopping off his head and turning him into delicious egg-lemon soup.

That rooster was an outlier. Most chickens are swell.

They certainly deserve a bit of luxury in exchange for providing my family with 75% of our protein intake — more on the weekends, when I don't have to throw away a bunch of cold scrambled eggs after dropping the kids off at school.

Then, add to that the bird flu that struck the nation's egg-laying hens last year, leading to the death of millions of chickens. That's not their fault, and if I have to pay more or eat something else for breakfast every now and then, that's OK with me.

A friend of mine recently posted on Facebook that she thought it would probably be cheaper to raise her own chickens than to buy eggs at the store.

That is untrue.

I know because I once researched raising chickens. Even after untangling the thousands of different breeds (would you like a Cream Legbar or a Rhode Island Red?), I balked after hitting pages of instructions for building a coop with sufficient access to dirt baths and grit, nesting boxes and heated poultry drinkers.

Plus, chicken-owners can't ever go on vacation. It's hard enough to find a babysitter, let alone someone trained to properly clean a dropping board.

Can you watch the chickens for a week while we go to Cabo? They don't need much, just water, food, bedding changes, sweeping, a little light coop cleaning. As long as they haven't been carried off by hawks when we get back, we'll be happy!

Plus, you haven't really encountered the harsh realities of home-raised chickens until you've visited Vieques in Puerto Rico. The island is an Eden full of white-sand beaches, but you awaken each morning (and midmorning and afternoon and late afternoon) to the sound of 5,000 roosters simultaneously airing their grievances loudly enough for the entire island to hear.

Who can blame the roosters, though? I'd be mad, too, if the U.S. Navy had been bombing my home for 60 years, to the point where there are so many unexploded ordinances that they can't safely clear away the underbrush to find all the unexploded ordinances.

(That, by the way, is true, though you may have never read about it before. It's certainly the kind of thing Ron DeSantis wouldn't want taught in schools, lest children ask the tricky question "Why?" in response.)

But back to the eggs.

Yes, buying them at the store has gotten expensive. But the other options — raiding my kids' college funds for coop maintenance, moving to Vieques and eating angry eggs all day — are no good, either.

For now, instead, I pay the price and lump it.

It's not that bad, really. It's certainly better than being chased around my backyard by an insecure rooster.

There's only so much egg-lemon soup a woman can eat.

Don Lemon Was Right; Nikki Haley Is Past Her Prime

February 18, 2023

Don Lemon, a moron, was right.

When Lemon got on his CNN show (I don't watch it. I don't know the name) and said that presidential candidate Nikki Haley, 51, was past "her prime," he was right.

He was right. There. I said it.

And when his co-host Poppy Harlow, recently nominated for the "Outstanding Work in Not Stabbing a Co-Host with Your Pen" Emmy, choked out a follow-up question — "Prime for what?" — Lemon took the honorable route and dodged.

"I'm just saying what the facts are. Google it."

Lemon didn't answer Harlow because the real answer, "her prime for sex," would be unseemly.

You see, Haley is in her 50s, and everyone knows — even, as Lemon pointed out, *Google* knows — that a woman's sexual prime is in her 20s, 30s, mayyyyyyybe 40s if she has stellar genes and/or imperceptible plastic surgery. After that, she's nothing more than an empty coconut husk, a dried-up flower, a shadowy relic of her former youth and glory.

You know it. I know it. Brave souls like Tucker Carlson and Ben Shapiro and another FOX News neckbeard whose name escapes me know it. Those three wise men recently pointed out that uncomfortable truth to comedian and bestselling author Chelsea Handler, who had made the grave mistake of saying that she, a childless woman, was happy.

As Carlson and Shapiro and Unnamed Neckbeard so gallantly informed her, though, Handler was not happy at all.

She was miserable.

She was nothing more than the sad, discarded pulp of an old Florida orange, squeezed dry of all its delicious nectar. And instead of putting that womanly juice to its only honorable use, childbearing, Handler had instead flushed it down the toilet of professional success and personal fulfillment.

Writing books? Hosting talk shows? Stand-up comedy? *Pshaw.*

None compares to procreation, which you know that Carlson and Shapiro and the rest of the GOP venerate above all other acts because they want absolutely no incentive for women to engage in it.

You know that conservatives truly treasure the contributions of mothers because they oppose, at every possible opportunity, anything that would make it easier to be one.

They don't want free health care for pregnant women but that's only because they love babies so much! They don't want paid parental leave but that's only because there's nothing as important as a mother's love! They don't want free school lunches for poor kids but that's only because a solid education is the best way out of poverty!

But never mind all of that.

You know Lemon was right about a 51-year-old woman being past her prime because he made his comments on the heels of a news cycle in which Madonna was dragged to hell and back for having refused to accept the demise of her primacy.

When she stepped on stage at the VMAs, forehead suspiciously unlined and lips mysteriously plump, it was a great insult to us all. Because Madonna is 64, long past her prime, and she should be dealing with that sad fact the only socially acceptable way possible, which is to hug her loved ones goodbye, step onto an ice floe and drift out into the ocean forever.

So, people, though it looks like Lemon's "inartful" comments may hasten his professional demise, though everyone's getting all hot and bothered about the suggestion that women's only feminine value is wired to a kind of biological bomb set to go off in their mid-40s, I say he deserves our thanks.

Thanks for pointing out what many older women don't realize, which is that their bodies belong, primarily, to their husbands, children and society at large, and only secondly, distantly, to themselves. Once they're too old to enjoy them, that is.

And if this all sounds cruel, I'm sorry. But don't shoot me. Don Lemon and I are just the messengers.

If You're Giving Away Bailouts, I'll Take One, Please

March 18, 2023

Dear Sirs (one assumes),

What follows is my official application to be included in the billions of dollars in bailouts — I'm sorry, "debt relief" — planned for the Silicon Valley banks that failed after engaging in risky tech industry loans, dumb cryptocurrency investments and faulty assumptions about interest rate hikes.

I have read recent reports that the federal government has already organized infusions of hundreds of billions of dollars into the banks to ensure their liquidity — in other words, to make certain that venture capitalists continue their unbroken streak of never facing the consequences of a bad investment.

Now, I am not a customer of these banks.

I am not the CEO of an eco-friendly swimsuit company or a totally legitimate service that delivers vegetables to your house and charges it to health insurance as medicine.

I do not own an "estate winery" that makes $200-a-bottle wine.

Nor do I run a company that speeds the movement of cryptocurrency, ensuring that shady transactions between anonymous accounts happen seamlessly, and that arms dealers, pornographers and heroin manufacturers can easily turn their unsecured digital Monopoly money into worthless cash.

I am just a loser mom, the CEO of My Home, Inc., and though I haven't been suffering as badly as the hedge funders who no longer can use their banks' Lake Tahoe ski retreats for free, I am also not doing as well, financially speaking, as I was pre-pandemic.

The consumer price index, or, in more technical terms, "what I pay for stuff" has increased between 2% and 10% over the last three years, and inflation is up 6% over a year ago. Now, I'm no treasury secretary, but that sounds bad.

Food manufacturers seem to think that customers won't notice if, instead of increasing the price, they just shrink the package to toddler portions. But then grocers figure, heck, why not just jack up the cost, too? Now, a box of cereal usually runs you $8 — about the same as an 8-pack of applesauce. Drown your sorrows in M&Ms and expect to pay as much as $13 a bag — on sale — for the privilege. Eggs? Well, the point has been made.

So, let me make a modest proposal: I will accept an infusion of liquidity to the tune of $100,000 — half the cost of one of the 300 wine events that a bank held in a year to persuade people to come borrow its money.

Now, you may balk at my proposal, thinking it's more important to allow bankers to continue to take their tech bro clients to race fancy sports cars.

Or maybe you think that, instead of helping me, the federal government should focus, despite the FDIC's "legal limit" of $250,000, on protecting the deposits of companies that kept $487 million, or a quarter of all their cash, undiversified, in one bank.

In response, I argue that it's a lot like corporate welfare to throw billions at banks that looked with benevolence upon their wealthy customers' harebrained startups, giving them chance after chance to make good, then cushioning their falls when the failure had been made clear.

I would suggest that preventing me, a regular person, from suffering a fiscal reckoning would be far less of a priority for the federal government and financial sector, the effect on me and my family be damned.

I might even go so far as to guess that if an average Joe Schmo went to his bank and said, "I've made some poor investments and can't pay my mortgage anymore," he would be treated with a coldness that would put an unheated California mountain ski lodge to shame.

In short, I'm sure there are some complex financial inner workings that I, a regular person who has never been flown to a human-made surf ranch at my banker's expense, do not understand.

But, frankly, I won't do anything dumber with the money than these banks did.

Think of it, if you like, as an investment.

If My Kids Ask About Trump, Here's What I'll Say

April 8, 2023

One day, I'll explain to my sons why Donald Trump was charged with a crime.

Well, 34 crimes, to be exact, but several alleged actions of increasing stupidity with just one aim: Hiding from the public his nature as an inveterate creep. Now, true, being a shameless philanderer isn't illegal, nor is paying someone off. But you know what is? Breaking laws, even boring little business fraud laws, to prevent further tarnish on your already poor reputation.

I don't think I'll have trouble explaining the case against Trump, which a New York grand jury found sufficiently compelling to issue an indictment.

But I might have to explain the critics.

Why, my sons could ask, did some conservatives freak out about it? I mean, isn't punishing crime, like, their whole deal?

First, I will explain to my boys that, though there was much Sturm und Drang about what infuriated Trumpites would do in response to Trump's arraignment, nothing serious came to pass. There were no huge protests. Trump wasn't dragged off in chains. The general public reacted with a shrug and a "wait and see." The only real noise came from political windbags.

Additionally, even before the charges against Trump had

been unsealed, a large majority — 60%, by one poll — supported the indictment, including 72% of independents.

The results lead one to believe that, perhaps, most Americans either suspected the charges had merit or trusted an impartial jury to determine that.

There were, though, a few noisy conservatives calling into question the charges' validity, saying that they're a kind of crossing-of-the-Rubicon moment from which the Democrats could never retreat.

We're coming after Democratic politicians now, they threatened. We're going to arrest every liberal lawbreaker.

To that, I say: Good!

If Democrats break the law, charge them. Charge them all!

If Joe Biden engages in criminal acts, present a case to a grand jury composed of his peers and get an indictment. Let him hire the best lawyers he can afford to defend himself. Allow him the chance to plead to a lesser crime, if he wishes, or have his day in court and hear a jury's verdict on his guilt or innocence. If he doesn't like the result, he can even appeal!

Frankly, it sounds exactly like what our criminal justice system should all be about.

But there was another subset of anti-indictment-istas, ones who gave a nod and a wink to Trump's behavior. Sure, he might have broken some laws, they seemed to say, but he's a former president, and you can't go around tossing them into prison for petty offenses.

Let he who has not had unprotected sex with a porn star and then later tried to buy her silence, hiding the nature of the transaction and attempting to delay payment until after the presidential election so he could safely renege — well, let that man cast the first stone!

I guess my response would be, OK, hand me the stones.

There's certainly a distinction to be made between immoral and illegal behavior, but Trump's alleged cheating (or even the supposed payoff) isn't the issue.

If he did what prosecutors say and fraudulently reported

the payment to cover up a violation of election law, it shouldn't matter how minor the infraction or how powerful the accused.

Thus far, no one has been able to successfully explain to me why the threshold for prosecution should be higher for a former president. Maybe that's because I live in Illinois, where we've prosecuted enough former (and current) elected officials to fill a high school graduating class.

If push comes to shove, I'll tell my kids this: Leniency may be granted but it's never owed. And Trump got as much leniency as he deserved.

What came next was up to the jury, and that was as it should be.

The Bizarre Failure of Conservatives To Quit When They're Ahead

June 3, 2023

June is Pride Month, so it's officially time for conservatives to lose their minds in an orgy of antigay bigotry not-that-convincingly disguised as traditional morality.

The influx of GOP rage directed at anything with a rainbow on it comes hot on the heels of an effort to take down Target for its Pride-themed merchandise. And *that* in turn arrives amid what seems like a never-ending tsunami of hatred for Bud Light's unpardonable sin of sending a personalized beer can to a trans social media influencer.

From the outside of all this, I can't figure out what conservatives have left to be mad about.

Bud Light folded like Superman on laundry day after the pushback for sending a beer can to influencer Dylan Mulvaney. The PR stunt was just one of many transparently craven attempts by corporations to link themselves to even the most tangentially famous young person. It's the kind of thing that happens all the time. Mulvaney — like it or not — has a fan base.

But once Bud Light's parent company, Anheuser-Busch, caught a whiff of blowback, they released a sniveling apology and put two executives in charge of the partnership on leave. Even if Republicans, for some reason, hate the idea of a company marketing itself to a trans influencer's fans so much that they'll (claim to) boycott every product that company makes, if they don't call off the boycott after it's successful, then they just come off looking like petulant babies who didn't really have any kind of sensible point in the first place. At least have the decency to take your ill-gotten gains and leave.

But no, there are still conservatives gleefully posting pictures of themselves on Twitter with non-Bud Light beers, which gives companies the message that even if they prostrate themselves completely to the conservative mob, they won't win. Why bother trying?

Just ask Target, which is still experiencing a similar rightwing firestorm simply for having rainbow-colored kids clothes with horrific statements on them like "I'm proud of you always" and "Just be you and feel the love."

At first, conservative protesters claimed to be offended that some of the available merchandise was designed by an artist who's created edgy, Satan-themed pieces outside of his partnership with Target. Well, Target pulled those designs. Then the complaints were that swimsuits designed for trans people were being marketed toward kids. Target pulled those, too. Now conservatives are just mad that there's anything even remotely LGBTQ-friendly anywhere in the stores.

It's a strange evolution for Republicans, who not that long ago seemed to understand that the whole point of running a business was to make a profit. Now that's seen as somehow gross and unethical, a perspective that sounds pretty liberal to me.

And as a self-avowed liberal, I'm a bit uncomfortable defending Target or Anheuser-Busch. I don't care if those gigantic companies do well, and I'm under no illusions that they've engaged in LGBTQ-friendly efforts for any reason other than to increase their stock prices. It's all hollow, corporate PR, but if it turns out that right-wingers took them too seriously, companies only have themselves to blame.

Here, though, is some free advice for conservatives: Ask yourselves what, exactly, you're trying to do with all these boycotts.

If it's "get companies to stop supporting LGBTQ people," then failing to stop pitching fits even after the companies melt like microwaved popsicles leads me to believe conservatives' tantrums will soon see diminishing returns.

But, if, as I suspect, the point of all this is just to rant nonsensically at anything vaguely progressive like a drunken uncle at Thanksgiving, then, well, I think noted conservative George W. Bush said it best a long time ago:

Mission accomplished.

No Real Point to Arguing About 'Try That In A Small Town'

July 22, 2023

Part of me feels like Jason Aldean has already gotten enough attention for his song, "Try That In A Small Town," which details how small-town vigilantes will shoot you for any number of infractions up to and including cussing at a cop or burning the flag.

But another, pushier part of me feels like there's more to be said.

I mean, honestly, Aldean must be reveling in the publicity, laughing himself sick as he watches his downloads shoot up with every angry tweet, op-ed and TikTok. It's been politicized at this point, and when country music stars get attacked by anyone or anything considered liberal, the target enjoys a resulting influx of conservative street cred.

"The ole Woke Police have got their claws in Aldean," Republicans say to themselves as they send more money to a filthy rich musician who's never lived in — heck, probably ever even visited — a small town.

It's all an effective illusion — this down-homey identity Alden (or, more likely, his team) has created.

Musicians are real people, but rest assured that their songs will reflect only the part of their identity that they want you to see.

If it sells more albums to be the kind of dude who uses his granddad's gun to dispense frontier justice to sidewalk sucker-punchers, then that's what he'll sing about.

Honestly, I'd never even heard of the "controversy" until Aldean himself tweeted about it.

"I'm so sick of people talking about this fire!" he seemed to say, pouring gasoline on it.

Now Americans are bickering about the ultimate culture conflict: small town vs. big city.

Well, I've lived in both, and, let me tell you, they both have advantages and disadvantages.

There's something comforting about being surrounded by people who know you — who know your parents and grandparents, who know where you went to high school and what kind of clothes you wore and the hairstyle you sported while you were there.

There's also something really creepy about it. The weight of the past can be oppressive, and it's hard to escape old judgments and expectations in a small town. Just by being different, you can wind up isolated and lonely.

But the big city isn't wall-to-wall awesomeness, either. There's callousness in anonymity, in being surrounded by so many who have no reason to care for you. I've watched folks literally step over a man lying out on the sidewalk. He might have been sick or, yes, he might have been drunk, but ultimately, those big-city people just had better things to do than get involved.

On the other hand, getting involved in a stranger's business doesn't always yield positive results. And with the sheer magnitude of souls in a big city, being weird isn't as, well, *weird* as it is in a small town. There's freedom, and opportunity, in the metropolis. And that's to say nothing of the restaurants.

Ultimately, though, this is just manufactured controversy.

Because no one thinks carjacking old ladies is fine, neither Aldean nor any of his GOP defenders have ever actually seen a real-life flag burning, and if you spit in a cop's face, you're getting arrested and charged with assaulting a police officer, regardless of the population size of the town for which the officer works.

The debate is fruitless: You either live in a small town or you don't. If you come from one, your experience there was good, bad or indifferent. No one's changing anyone's mind.

It's like arguing about how many angels can dance on the head of a pin: Even if we find the right answer, so what?

Like so many skirmishes in the culture war, it's just a distraction from anything that counts, anything that can truly help or hurt us.

It's entertainment, in a way, and if the cage match of small town versus big city doesn't entertain you, I say it's perfectly fine to see your way out.

From here on out, that's what I'm doing, anyway.

Now that I've had the luxury of having my say.

Acknowledgments

Thank you to everyone who's contributed in large ways or small to the writings in this book, including Tim, Christian, Georgie, George, Nancy, Demetri, Chris, Laurie and Rick, Amy and Molly, Lizzie and Kevin, and Ricky and Cindy. Thank you to team at Creators Syndicate for publishing this book and for syndicating my column. Thank you to the many excellent editors I've had over the years, including Dan Lambert and Alex Nagy. Thank you to those who've told me (and, more importantly, others) that they like my columns — a group that includes Johnny K., Karen Cullotta and the many readers of The Villages Daily Sun. And thank you to all the people in this wonderful world who try their best to be kind. There are more of us than there are of them, and don't you ever forget it.

About the Author

Georgia Garvey is a former newspaper reporter and editor whose work has run in the Chicago Tribune, the L.A. Times, the Boston Globe and the Pioneer Press, among others. She now works as a writer and editor out of a fantastic old house in Illinois that her husband (who has to fix everything) likes a lot less than she does. Every February, she considers moving to a place where your eyelashes don't freeze on the way to the car, and every June, she asks herself why anyone would ever want to leave the Midwest.

Georgia is a first-generation Greek immigrant, a factoid of which she is certain to inform you within five minutes of sitting down next to her. It continues to interest her that, growing up, she was considered an American in Greece and a Greek in America.

Her column, distributed by Creators Syndicate, runs in publications across the country. Georgia has won several awards for her column-writing and is certain that, we re awards granted for the parenting of two small children who are smarter than she is, she would have gotten at least an honorable mention there as well. Honestly, shouldn't we all?

Everything Is Going To Be OK (Until It's Not)

is also available as an e-book
for Kindle, Amazon Fire, iPad, Nook and
Android e-readers. Visit creatorspublishing.com
to learn more.

CREATORS PUBLISHING

We find compelling storytellers and help them craft their narrative, distributing their novels and collections worldwide.

Made in the USA
Monee, IL
19 September 2023

42979141R00184